THE TEACH YOURSELF BOOKS

SQUASH RACKETS

TEACH YOURSELF

SQUASH
RACKETS

LESLIE HAMER
and
REX BELLAMY

THE ENGLISH UNIVERSITIES PRESS LIMITED
ST. PAUL'S HOUSE   WARWICK LANE
LONDON E.C.4

First printed 1968

SBN 340 05987 7
Printed and Bound in Great Britain for the English
Universities Press Ltd. by Butler & Tanner Ltd.,
Frome and London

Foreword

by Jonah Barrington

In 1966–67 Barrington, a Cornish-born Irish international, became only the second player—and the first from Great Britain—to win both the open and amateur championships in the same season. In 1967–68 he repeated the feat.

It has given me considerable pleasure to provide a foreword for this admirable book. I have been "in" squash for a comparatively short period of time, and I have had the great good fortune to meet many excellent people connected with the game. Rex Bellamy and Leslie Hamer come at once into this category. Both have, in their different ways, made a most valuable contribution to squash rackets. However in this book they have undoubtedly excelled themselves. The literary "marriage" of the journalist and the squash professional has produced in my opinion one of the most thorough and stimulating technical books to date.

We are now at a stage where squash rackets has a decidedly international flavour, and the game is developing at an almost alarming pace. I use the word "alarming" advisedly in that with this tremendous growth, particularly in playing numbers, we are now faced with the distinct problem of limited playing facilities and even less practical coaching. All the top professionals are attached to clubs, which restricts their coaching scope. Therefore to be provided with such a comprehensive, detailed examination of all aspects of the game as this book supplies can do nothing but good, not only for those starting to participate but also for the better exponent.

Rex Bellamy is generally accepted throughout the world as the leading squash writer of the day. He is so accurately informative that one might well expect Rex to have played the game for many years. However he was a comparative late

starter and was at one time in the invidious position of having
to provide comment without any real depth of personal experience. That he is now considered such an authority on
squash, at all levels, pays tribute to his intense enthusiasm
for the sport and inevitably his dedication to the task of
educating himself in the mysteries and complications of the
game. The Bellamy humour, always so very perceptive and
spontaneous, is now an indispensable feature of the squash
world. His articles during the major championships are
always eagerly awaited and never fail to stimulate the
"cognoscenti".

For almost thirty years attached to the well-known Bath
Club, not only is Leslie Hamer one of Britain's best-liked
professionals but probably one of the most knowledgeable
and experienced in his art. Players of all standards have
benefited from his methodical and always genuine approach
to the game of squash. By means of the excellent diagrams,
he puts on paper his ideas on the basic technique of stroking
the ball, and to this he adds many valuable views on the
competitive and tactical aspects of squash rackets. Leslie's
knowledge has been acquired over many years of playing,
watching and talking about the game. He has certainly
travelled the world with a squash racket—for three years he
was the squash professional on a world-cruising liner. He
has for many years been involved in the administration of
the game and in fact was secretary of the professionals'
committee for an extensive period.

This completely professional partnership has I feel
produced a most necessary professional book. Not the least
of the varied accomplishments of the authors is their very
proud boast of being two of the few who have actually
played squash in Japan. This startling coincidence, although
remarkable, is not the most significant of their qualifications
for writing a book about the game. But it is well in character
with the uninhibited nature of their quest for the truth about
squash.

The Authors

Leslie Hamer has been a squash coach since 1929 and his experience is unsurpassed. He has been playing and teaching the game all his working life—first at Marlborough College, then aboard R.M.S. *Franconia* (Cunard Line), at Thames House S.R.C. (at that time the largest in the world), and, since 1937, at Mayfair's famous Bath Club, one of the West End social clubs traditionally regarded as the game's spiritual home. He has conducted S.R.A. and C.C.P.R. coaching courses and has served on four of the most important S.R.A. committees: championship; referees, markers, and rules; professionals; and technical. He played for the British professional team during their 1964 tour of the United States and Canada, and has twice captained the professionals in their annual match with the amateurs.

Rex Bellamy is the foremost writer on the game. He had his first squash lesson from an R.S.M. at Sandhurst, was founder-secretary of *The Times* S.R.C., and is a member of West Wycombe Squash Club. He has been a sports journalist since 1944, working in Sheffield and Birmingham until he joined *The Times* in 1956. One of Fleet Street's most accomplished and versatile reporters, he has no superiors in his special fields—squash and tennis. A member of the Sports Writers' Association, the Association Internationale de la Presse Sportive, and the Lawn Tennis Writers' Association.

The authors share an unusual distinction. Both have played squash in Japan—Mr. Hamer when the *Franconia* anchored at Yokohama one day in the 30s, Mr. Bellamy when he played on the British Embassy court during the 1964 Olympic Games in Tokyo.

Acknowledgements

The authors are grateful for the kind co-operation of the Squash Rackets Association and the International Squash Rackets Federation; to Mr. John Horry, who is secretary of both, for his help and advice; and to Mr. Jonah Barrington for contributing a foreword.

Contents

	page
Foreword	v
The Authors	vii
Acknowledgements	viii
Introduction: *What are we playing at?— How it happened—The way ahead*	I
A Bloodless Substitute	13
It's in the Bag: *Clothes—Socks—Shoes— Women's wear—Racket—Ball*	16
Courts	23
The Language of the Game	27
The Rules of Squash Rackets	35
The Grip	48
Footwork	51
Forehand: *Preparation—Impact—Follow-through*	53
Backhand	57
Length	59
Service	62
Angle	70
Reverse Angle	74
Boast: *Single boast—Double boast—Back-wall boast*	77
Drop Shot	83
Volley	88
Half-volley	92
Lob	94
Spin: *Cut—Slice*	97
Return of Service	101

Match Play: *Reconnaissance—The knock-up—
Begin at the beginning—Central station—
Everything in its place—Strength to strength—
How goes the enemy?—He who runs may read—
Pianoforte—Intent to deceive—Never turn your
back—The con man—The inquest*   110

Etiquette   126
Look and Learn   131
Fitness and Practice   134
Useful Information   145

List of Figures

		page
1	The court	24
2	Forehand grip	49
3	Backhand grip	49
4	Length shot (forehand)	60
5	Length shot (backhand)	61
6	Length service	64
7	Side wall service	65
8	Lob service	65
9	"Hammer" service	67
10	Midcourt service	67
11	Correctly played angle	72
12	Wrongly played angle	72
13	Backhand reverse angle	75
14	Forehand boast	78
15	Wrongly played boast	79
16	Lob service	80
17	Drop shot "box"	85
18	Service and returns	102
19	Service and returns	105
20	Service and returns	107
21	Back-wall angle	108
22	Routes to and from corners	129
23	Service practice (2 players)	137
24	Angle practice (6 or 7 players)	138
25	Practice (3 players)	139
26	Reverse angle practice (2 players)	140
27	Practice (3 players)	141
28	Practice (4 players)	142

List of Plates

Between pages 52/53

1(a) Jonah Barrington (Britain)
1(b) Cameron Nancarrow (Australia)
2(a) Dick Carter (Australia)
2(b) Aftab Jawaid (Pakistan)
3(a) Jonah Barrington (Britain)
3(b) Ken Hiscoe (Australia)
4(a) Ken Hiscoe (Australia)
4(b) Geoff Hunt (Australia)

Between pages 84/85

5 Heather McKay (Australia)
6 Heather McKay (Australia)
7 Ibrahim Amin (Egypt) and David Brazier (Britain)
8 Dick Carter (Australia) and Aftab Jawaid (Pakistan)

Introduction

Kipling wrote that "Allah created the English mad—the maddest of all mankind!" But the Irish, Scottish, and Welsh are afflicted by the same malady (the relatively sober Scots, remember, gave us golf, an incredibly complicated ritual for deciding who shall pay for the drinks . . .). The British as a whole have always had a national genius—and genius, it is said, is akin to madness—for inventing games, and a national compulsion for playing them. So they acquired an unparalleled network of games for all tastes and all weathers. And every game was exported by the Services and by emigrants during the expansion of the British Empire. Now the Empire has gone: but Britain's infectious madness for playing games finds an enthusiastic response from every nation in the world. The British may still be "the maddest of all mankind". But there are some pretty close runners-up, not least the descendants of British settlers in Australia, New Zealand, and South Africa.

Yet the national compulsion for playing games soon struck a snag, since games were traditionally played outdoors—and Britain has a climate that the cynical describe as "eight months of winter and four months of bad weather". This was a challenge to the national genius for invention, and the British came up with a peculiar assortment of indoor games. Squash was the best of them. In the decade preceding the preparation of this book, the manufacturers' figures for the sales of British sports equipment showed clearly enough which way the trend was heading: in terms of percentage increases, squash had advanced more than twice as fast as any other sport, indoor or outdoor. In that decade, the sales figures for squash gear had more than doubled. Nor was the boom limited to the rank and file. For the decade ended with a historic triumph, at the very summit of the game, by a Cornishman called Jonah Barrington, who became the first British player in the history of the game to win the open and amateur championships in the same season. The nation of its birth was once more leading the way as squash roared ahead in the popularity polls throughout the world. All of which brings us to the question . . .

What are we playing at?

First of all, squash is played in a pit 32 ft. long and 21 ft. wide. The front wall is 15 ft. high, the back wall 7 ft. high, so that the side walls are 8 ft. higher at the front of the court than they are at the back. The upper limits of the side walls sink gradually from front to back, like a descending line on a graph. So that you can get in and out of the court without using a ladder, a door fits flush into the back wall. Basically the game is a little like lawn tennis—except that both players are on the same side of the "net", which in this case is a strip of metal, known as the "tin", at the bottom of the front wall. The players have a racket each and take it in turns to hit a small, soft black ball above the tin. The ball must go over the tin before touching the floor. Then the other player can volley it, or allow it to bounce once. He loses the rally if he allows the ball to bounce more than once—or hits it into the tin; or onto the walls on or above the lines marking the upper limits of the court; or onto the lights or any other fittings in the roof. A point can be scored only by the player who is serving. When he loses a rally, he loses the right to serve (the excellence of this system is that the player who is serving can be as adventurous as he likes in choosing his shots, because a mistake will not cost him a point). The basic idea is that the first player to score nine points wins a game, and the first player to win three games wins the match. But if a game reaches 8-all, the player who is *not* serving can decide whether the game will go to the first man to win another point, or to the first man to win two more points. So the farthest any game can go is 10-9.

A game is started by a player standing with at least one foot in a service box and not touching any of the lines around it. At the beginning of a match the right to serve is decided by spinning a racket. The server may start from either box, but after winning each point he must change over to the other box. The server throws the ball up and hits it direct onto the front wall. The ball must hit the front wall above a line (called the "cut line") marked across it, and then rebound over the "short line" (painted across the floor) into the opponent's half-court—though the opponent may, if he chooses, return the ball before it bounces. After hitting the front wall, the service may touch any other wall before it bounces into the opponent's half-court. The receiver must return the ball before it has bounced twice, so that it hits the front wall anywhere above the tin. But the service is the only stroke that has to be hit *direct* onto the front wall. Any other stroke in a rally can be cannoned off another wall, so long as it eventually hits the front wall above the tin before bouncing. Apart from the service, it does not matter where the ball bounces. So a rally goes on until one player puts the ball into the tin or out of court, or allows it to bounce twice.

There are four basic shots—the drive, the drop shot, the lob, and the angle (with its brother, the boast). The first three are similar to the same strokes in lawn tennis. But the angle and boast are strokes played onto a side wall so that the ball rebounds onto the front wall. The ball may even be cannoned off two or three other walls before it hits the front wall. But once the ball leaves the racket, it must not bounce until it has struck the front wall. It is the variety of side-wall shots (plus the fact that squash is the only popular game in which both players are on the same side of the "net") that gives squash its special appeal. The presence of the walls also means that even novices can put every service into court without difficulty, and can then keep the rallies going for a long time.

All this may seem a rather strange basis for the fastest growing sport of our time. But give it a try: and the boom will soon explain itself. Squash can be played by either sex, at any age, at any time, in any weather. It asks no favours of the climate. It ignores rain and darkness outside. For boys and girls, men and women, whether 16 or 60, it offers concentrated competitive exercise—and exercise that is as absorbing for the mind as it is healthy for the body. Its nature can be adjusted to the needs of the individual: its pace gentle or fierce, its texture delicate or strong. At its highest level all these qualities mingle, even in the course of one rally—the quick and the slow, the violent and the cunning. The only prerequisite for an exciting and satisfying match is that the two players concerned should have a similar ability. Even if this condition is not met, pleasant exercise is still available, as long as the better player directs his shots to areas where they will not be too difficult for his opponent to retrieve.

For the novice, the game's rewards are immediate, since squash permits rapid progress—up to a point—for anyone with even a modest ball sense. After only a few hours on court, two beginners will know enough to have a vigorous and enjoyable match. Later the game's mask of simplicity falls away. But a glittering treasure house stands revealed: a treasure house in which the lightning of sudden shafts of speed flickers around the caressing brushwork of deception. Where all seemed straightforward, the novice, in wonderment, finds himself in a furiously complicated world where geometry becomes a game, where animal energy is married to the mental agility of the chessboard. He is playing "physical chess"—fighting a battle of wits, at high speed. In short, squash can be as simple, or as complex, as you care to make it.

Squash is perfectly in tune with the tempo of the modern age. It only asks an hour of our time, the hour including the whole process of changing, playing, taking a shower, and changing back again. In that hour anyone can take exactly as much exercise as he or she wants—no more, and no less. No time is wasted by trotting off to fetch the ball when it has been hit out of court—the walls do the fetching for us. The game is cheap to play, and in terms of fitness alone offers a dazzling investment all the year round. But the young may prefer it as a complement to some outdoor game, and in this respect, too, squash is superb. It tones up the whole system, sharpens reflexes, improves coordination of hand and eye, and does not neglect a muscle. If there is a cricketer or a lawn tennis player, a footballer or a rugby player, who says squash is no use to him, then he has never played the game.

Like a good party, squash is congenial and noisy (when two good players are in action, a court can sound like a pistol range). Whether we play in some remote corner of the provinces, or in the spacious comforts of the West End social clubs, squash provides companionship of a quality that few sports can equal and none can surpass. Whatever we may ask of a game, squash has all the answers: and those answers make us a little healthier, a little more alert, a little more considerate, a little better equipped for our everyday lives. We can expect no more from any sport.

How it happened

In the days before shops, when our ancestors had either to grow their food or catch it, there was no need to invent games. The tricky business of staying alive was enough to keep them on their toes. But as the need for these primitive pursuits receded, sport began to develop, notably the elementary exercise of running. Later came ball games, in all their ramifications. We started knocking the ball at each other, or against a wall ("Fives", denoting the fingers of one hand, is still with us). Then, as the richly diverse texture of sport became woven into the pattern of history, an odd assortment of rackets came into use. In the 19th century the famous public school at Harrow, just outside London, was already a thriving centre for the old game of rackets (still played, on a small scale). From this emerged the germ of the game we now call squash rackets, which outgrew its parent long ago. So the place of birth was Harrow. The date of birth? There can be no specific answer. All that can safely be said is that squash evolved as an informal variant of rackets (one of the walls used was the outside of the rackets court), about the middle of the 19th century. There were a series of makeshift courts, accidental rather than deliberate in their structure. In the late 1860s, and the 1870s, the first vague, tentative steps were made towards a standard court. The word "squash" was also becoming accepted. Unlike its parent game of rackets, the variant was played with a soft, hollow ball (sometimes with holes in it) that "squashed" and made appropriate noises when it hit the walls. In 1883 the first court designed specifically for squash was built by a Harrow man, at Oxford. By 1886 squash was beginning to achieve some sort of recognition as an independent game. In succeeding decades, courts were built in private dwellings and in the London social clubs (still the game's spiritual home). Squash was growing up.

The Tennis and Rackets Association (formed in 1907)—and we should point out that the tennis was the "royal" or "real" game played indoors, as distinct from lawn tennis—appointed a sub-committee to draw up some rules for squash and administer the game. In 1911 the Association laid down standard measurements for squash courts, but these did not take their final shape until after the 1914–18 War. Early in the twenties came the first national championships for men and women, though the United States

(1906), South Africa (1910), and Canada (1911) had got off the mark a lot sooner. The Squash Rackets Association had an inaugural meeting in 1928, became officially established a year later, and took over the administration of the game from the Tennis and Rackets Association (the three sports remain inseparably linked by the common denominator of indoor courts, though squash quickly outstripped the other two in popularity). Associations had been formed in the United States (1907) and Canada (1911): but in spite of the fact that they used the word "squash", our friends across the Atlantic played with a hard ball on a slightly different type of court, so that their game developed on vastly contrasting lines from its English counterpart. In retrospect, this was a lamentable digression, since it meant that the Americans and Canadians had backed the wrong horse. They developed a game that fell midway between squash and rackets and therefore left them out on a limb—playing a game that had taken root nowhere else. Nowadays the American and Canadian game has no more in common with British squash than British squash has with rackets, or rugby union with rugby league. But one overseas nation backed the *right* horse, because in 1910 South Africa formed an association who promoted the British game as distinct from the American.

With the S.R.A. fully in control of an expanding young game, the 1930s were boom years. The manufacture of a slower ball made the technique of squash both more subtle and more spectacular. It became far more skilful and strenuous than its counterpart across the Atlantic. The whole technical and tactical scope of the game was adjusted and expanded, and this inevitably marked the last break with rackets, which had given squash its first players and its first administrators. The Women's S.R.A. was formed in 1934. Squash clubs sprang up everywhere. More overseas countries began to take up the game. The seeds took root in Australia, though in those days no one could have guessed that, a quarter of a century later, Australia would lead the world in a startling exploitation of the commercial possibilities of vast blocks of public courts, where anyone could play at any time (there are now more courts in Sydney than in any other city in the world).

In squash, as in so many other spheres of human endeavour, the 1939–45 War was an interregnum. Afterwards came a huge leap forward, with squash fast becoming a world game. The 1950s were great years. It was then that the boom really hit Australia (within 10 astonishing years they sprang from obscurity to achieve a higher overall standard than any other nation). It was then that the wondrous family of Pathans, the Khans, lifted the game to a new plane. It was then that British schools began to shake off their traditional prejudice against individual as opposed to team games, so that squash (like lawn tennis) became an increasingly respectable part of the sporting curriculum. The game pushed its roots through the entire community. Squash was no longer the almost exclusive prerogative of public schoolboys and West End social clubs. All this was exciting, because if the apex of the pyramid is to be high, then the base must be broad. But perhaps the chief reason for the game's breakneck advance, everywhere, was the many special qualities that made it perfectly adjusted to the bustling, quick-thinking tempo of modern life. Competition became fiercer, international rivalry more intense. Tours multiplied. Every season contingents of rugged, superbly trained players from overseas came to London for the big championships. With a few individual exceptions, the British game was not geared to competition of this fervour. From a playing point of view the parent nation of squash seemed to be in its dotage. The Australians and Egyptians came to the fore, contrasted in style but equally dedicated to success. From overseas came rumblings of discontent. Why should the world's best players always have to travel to London for the "world" championships? Why should

Britain administer the game when they could no longer set the pace on court? The criticisms were soundly based. The young players of overseas nations—players not yet good enough to earn an expensive trip to London—needed and deserved the inspiration of watching the world's best players on their own courts. And so far as its administration was concerned, squash had clearly become too big a sport for one national association to handle.

Fortunately the S.R.A. had appointed, in 1955, a secretary whose diplomacy and unparalleled knowledge of the game were to serve them well when the crisis came. Mr. John Horry did not allow the discontent to grow. With foresight and initiative, he and his colleagues on the S.R.A. drew together the scattered threads of the world game. Thus the post-war expansion led, in January, 1966, to an international conference in London. The delegates decided to form the International Squash Rackets Federation, to take over responsibility for the rules of the game, to coordinate tours, and to settle any international disputes. They also decided that the first official world team and individual championships would be played in Australia in August, 1967 (Geoff Hunt led Australia to both the team and individual titles). The constitution drawn up at that conference was ratified during 1966 by the seven founder members—Australia, Great Britain, India, New Zealand, Pakistan, South Africa, and the United Arab Republic. In January, 1967, the newly-born I.S.R.F. held their inaugural meeting in London. Britain provided the offices and the officers. But the S.R.A. were now no more than the first among equals. As in so many other sports that Britain gave to the world, the time had come to admit that the family had grown up. The game had begun yet another new era.

The way ahead

Squash has now become the victim of its own virtues. There are not enough courts for the people who want to play.

There is not enough room for the people who want to watch.
In Britain, commercial speculators and local authorities
probably hold the key to the future in the way of providing
new courts, since the prime need is for public as distinct
from private courts. These would also raise the level of
Britain's national team by broadening the basis of recruit-
ment. A national ranking list, as in lawn tennis, would be
another incentive for those players prepared to work at the
game instead of merely playing at it. Standards could also
be improved—and inevitably will be—by a longer and
stronger competitive season, with inter-club and inter-
county competitions achieving a higher status. The advent
of an itinerant world championship may help indirectly, by
reducing overseas participation in the two British championships to such an extent that it will no longer be necessary to sandwich them together, in December and January.
This was done in order that overseas players could compete
in both during one trip to London. But (except in years
when the world championship is played in London) it may
now be possible to strengthen the British season by holding
one championship in the middle and the other towards the
end.

The task of exploiting the game's remarkable visual
appeal—squash is packed with action, in a confined space,
with no longueurs—has been baffling. For one thing the
nature of the pit-like court has made it impossible to
accommodate more than 200 to 300 spectators (and most
of those cannot see *all* the court) on steeply banked tiers of
seats above and behind the walls of the court. The camera
suggested an alternative, if not an answer. But the difficulties
facing the film-makers were immense. These fell basically
into two spheres—first, definition (picking out the flight of
a fast-moving black ball against the background of a dark
brown floor); second, camera positions. The Australians
have been particularly resourceful in tackling these problems, and, with the aid of several cameras, have succeeded

in televising matches "live" to paying customers on adjacent courts. Nowadays the big championships in London are also filmed, though they have yet to be televised "live". The real answer must be courts specially constructed to meet the needs of the camera—and in 1966 such a court was built at Birkenhead. This had a back wall containing a section made of glass, 18 ft. by 5 ft., through which matches could be filmed. Clearly the camera is gradually over-coming an exciting but awkward challenge. But the question of accommodating more spectators is apparently insoluble. After all, how many people can watch what is happening in a small pit? An all-glass court (a mammoth fish tank!) with one-way vision seems, at the moment, to be a wildly expensive dream from the realm of science fiction. Perhaps something may be contrived with mirrors. But for the time being it seems that squash must remain a paradox—the first popular game that cannot be watched by large crowds . . . a glorious spectator sport that few spectators can watch. . .

A further problem is that although squash has reached its centenary and is now booming all over the world, the boom is still largely confined to the countries of the old Empire days. The game would spread wider, faster, if it were not so difficult for other interested nations to try it out, to see what they think of it. The handicap here is that the traditional squash court is an expensive permanent structure costing as much as a house. But there are hopeful signs. Any boom in public interest means that there is a market to be tapped, and when this situation arises, commercial interests—quick to see the possibilities of squash—are naturally reluctant to regard any obstacle as insuperable. The basic need to produce more courts quickly, in order to satisfy an existing demand that far outstrips supply, has led the manufacturers' research down some interesting byways. Prefabricated courts are now on the market. So are relatively cheap collapsible wooden courts, suitable for

instruction and demonstrations (these may answer the
needs of those countries in eastern Europe, and elsewhere,
who want to have a look at the game). For all the difficulties
that beset the game now, and will continue to beset it in
the future, there is no knowing where the advance of
squash will end. It is expanding fast through every community who already have facilities for playing it. Within a
decade it may have crossed so many frontiers that it will be
knocking on the door for admittance to the Olympic
programme.

A Bloodless Substitute

"Books are good enough in their own way", wrote Stevenson, "but they are a mighty bloodless substitute for life." This quotation merely introduces the advice that what we preach here needs to be practised on court. To make the most of this book, go through it slowly and turn every piece of written knowledge into practical reality on court. If you can do so with the aid of a professional—or, failing that, an experienced and accomplished player—so much the better. This aid, if you can get it, will be particularly valuable at the beginning of your squash career, when you are choosing a racket and learning the right way to grip it. If you can afford it, take professional advice in the basics of the game, because faults in technique are difficult to uproot once they become firmly planted. If you cannot get a professional, but experienced players are available to advise you, take care in choosing your man. Because there are many fine players—even at the game's highest level—whose games have individual peculiarities they may pass on to you. Most professionals—even if you cannot afford to take lessons from them—will tell you whether the player you have in mind is or is not a good model. If no advice is available, use the book carefully and thoroughly until such time as a good tutor comes your way (this should not be long, because the S.R.A. are now grooming qualified amateur coaches in increasing numbers).

We suggest you read the whole book first, so that you get a rough overall picture of what is in store for you. Then go back to the beginning and take the book chapter by chapter, practising each new shot on court. The advice is all addressed to right-handed players, but if you are a left-hander you are probably already accustomed to reading "right" for "left" and so on. The forehand and backhand drives are the basic strokes, so make sure that you get these properly organized. The side walls will give you some baffling experiences at first. It will take time for you to work out the geometric possibilities they offer, notably as a means of drawing your opponent to the forecourt. But keep at it. Side wall strokes are among the most satisfying in the game, and you will soon get the hang of them. If you can, watch some good players in action and work out what they are trying to do. They will give you an idea of the road to follow. When on court yourself, watch the ball, particularly while your opponent is hitting it, and keep your wrist flexible (as opposed to the locked wrist of lawn tennis). Hit low—no more than 6 in. above the tin—when you are playing attacking shots. Remember that the important thing is the ability to put the ball where you want it, and that all the strokes (whether elegant or not) are only a means to this end. If you are a schoolboy, and under 18, why not measure your progress by having a crack at getting the S.R.A. junior proficiency certificate? There are practical and oral examinations at three levels—elementary, intermediate, and advanced.

Squash is mostly played with the head of the racket "open" (that is, with the bottom edge of the head farther forward than the top edge). Occasionally you hit "flat", with the head of the racket vertical. You seldom need a "closed" head (with the top edge farther forward than the bottom edge) because top spin is hardly ever used in squash. Our illustrations should help you to get the right idea about this and other fundamentals. So should the chapter on "The Language of the Game". Throughout your months as a novice this book will be an invaluable guide and reference; and even when your game has matured there will still be much here to refresh your thinking about the game, or to help you straighten out a stroke that suddenly begins to let you down.

In short, don't expect us to fight your battles for you— but use the book as a teacher and come back to it as a friend.

It's in the Bag

In terms of equipment, the basic requirements for a game of squash are simple enough—racket, balls, shirt or singlet, shorts, sweater or cardigan, socks, shoes, and towel. Most of these are obvious. A sweater is necessary because temperatures vary: some courts are cold, some warm; and players, like cars, tend to start cold. So a sweater is useful at the beginning of a game, while you are warming up, and again at the end, while you are cooling down on the way to the shower. The insistence on a shower may puzzle that starry-eyed innocent, the genuine beginner. Have no illusions. If you do not sweat when playing squash, you are not trying; if you do sweat, you will need a shower; and if you need a shower, you need a towel. So make sure it's in the bag with the rest of the stuff. If you are blatantly overdue at the barber's, or wear glasses, a head band might be useful—to keep your hair out of the way or stop sweat from dripping onto your glasses. A head band could also put your opponent out of his stride, since it will make you look like a Red Indian. But on the whole they are worn by women rather than men. A sweat band for your racket wrist is not a bad idea. It will keep your hand free of sweat running down from the forearm, and you can also use it for wiping your forehead. Buy the best equipment you can afford. Take particular care over your choice of racket, shoes, and socks, because careless purchases will be bad for your game and bad for your feet.

Clothes

In general, tennis clothes are equally suitable for squash. As in tennis, their colour should be predominantly white, though women often allow themselves bright little embellishments in the way of bandeaux or decorated hems. Dark colours are unfair because they make it difficult for your opponent to keep sight of the black ball (just as the opposite is true in table tennis). Shorts and the Wimbledon type of shirt are ideal. There is a lot of twisting, turning, and stretching to do—plenty of "stop" and "go"—in a game of squash. Freedom of movement is essential, and if your clothes are tight, sweat will make them stick to the skin and hamper you: to achieve comfort and mobility, avoid tight-fitting clothes. Do not be tempted by any of the modern materials that cannot absorb sweat. To sum up, choose clothes that are comfortable and fit snugly without being tight, and make sure that the materials are absorbent. Keep them clean and properly pressed: the better you look, the better you feel—and the better you feel, the better you play.

Socks

These are almost a question of trial and error—but we will help you to learn from the trials and errors of others. Again, you want something that will soak up the sweat, so choose the material carefully and avoid thin socks. Thick, cushion-foot socks are the most suitable, since they are absorbent and comfortable. Some players prefer two pairs of thin socks to one pair of thick socks, and this is something you will have to find out for yourself. At the first sign of tenderness or blisters, try something different. It would be inviting trouble, a guarantee of blisters, to wear socks that had not been washed since they were last used. As to size and fit, your toes must have room for free movement. The balance and ease with which you twinkle about the court depend on the flexibility your toes are allowed. Squash demands the footwork of the dance hall rather than the running track.

Shoes

Black-soled shoes are banned, because more often than not they mark the court, and the marks are difficult to erase. In the dressing room, or on the door of the court, you will find a notice to the effect that black-soled shoes are not permitted. Again, comfort is important—and that means enough room to move your toes about. So give yourself a feeling of freedom, as long as the shoes are not like barges (this can be dangerous—if you try to bustle about the court in shoes that are too big, there may be many a painful stumble, the potential consequences ranging from sprained ankles to concussion). The aim is a pair of shoes that will enable you to be both quick-footed and sure-footed. And be careful with the lacing. Players who lace their shoes too tightly always suffer from blisters or painful feet (sure signs of a "tenderfoot" in the novice sense). You never meet a professional who plasters his feet or is bothered by hard or tender skin—yet they play almost all day and every day. The thing is that they never play in tight shoes, they take care with the lacing, and they know how to choose socks. The weight of the shoes is largely a matter of choice, but there are several factors to bear in mind. Because of all the stretching and twisting they have to do, the shoes must be flexible, strong, and well made. Because fleetness of foot is imperative, they must not be too heavy. The cushion-type sole is essential, but it must not be too thick: in this respect the normal tennis shoe may be unsuitable.

Women's wear

The general principles governing men's squash clothes apply to women's clothes too. There are certain points of detail worth noting. First of all, nothing should fit so tightly round the midriff that it restricts freedom of movement. As for hair styles, a bandeau (head band) is an effective and attractive method of keeping long hair out of the way. At the other end of the outfit, many women wear two pairs of socks, since their feet tend to blister more easily than men's. A choice has to be made between shorts, skirt, or dress. Shorts are more businesslike, since they do not obstruct the stroke, or the opponent's view of the ball. But not every woman looks good in shorts. If you feel more comfortable in a skirt or dress, do not wear one that is flared, since this would get in the way of your strokes. This brings us to a few more delicate areas of advice on which the authors have sought guidance from those better qualified to give it. As the game involves a lot of bending, pants must be neatly fitted and adequate for the purpose. There is no excuse for either discomfort or embarrassment, since sportswear manufacturers know that something special is required and have adapted their designs accordingly. It would be no service to the fair sex if we were too coy to share the fruits of our enquiries, on your behalf, about brassières: stretch straps are essential, and remember to pop some safety pins in your bag. Shoulder straps have a habit of snapping under the stress and strain of squash. Even in championships, competitors occasionally disappear for repairs . . .

Racket

This is probably the most expensive item on the newcomer's shopping list, but it is also the most important. The framework of the head must be wooden, but the shaft may be made of steel, glass-fibre, cane, or, of course, various laminations of wood. When you have decided how much you can afford to pay, the choice of a racket becomes a matter of individual preference. Handle every type of racket available, go through the motions of swinging at a ball, and find out which racket feels most comfortable. If you can do this with the advice of a professional or a top-class player, so much the better. There are a few points to keep in mind. The heavier the racket, the more hard wear it will stand and the longer it will last (assuming you don't tread on it, try to thump holes in the wall, or use it for beating carpets). Many steel-shafted rackets feel rather solid and for that reason are probably not the best choice for a player with a weak wrist. Glass-fibre and cane-shafted rackets usually feel lighter and have more whip. With lots of use they can even become too whippy, which means that the head of the racket will be behind the shaft as you follow through with the stroke. But these shafts do stand up to reasonably hard wear. Watch the stringing—it should not be too tight. A tennis racket is not the most reliable of guides here, because the head of a squash racket is small and the ball is light: this means that a tightly strung racket will be of no advantage (perhaps the opposite —you may lose the "feel" that controlled stroke-making demands). Look after your racket, which can be ruined by dampness. When you are not using it, keep it in a press. As for the grip (the covering on the shaft-handle), this can be of towelling (easily replaced when dirty), leather (which has resin in it), or rubber. If your hand sweats freely, the towelling grip may be best; or you may prefer leather (if you have a small, weak hand, you do not want a thick grip). If your hand remains dry in spite of exertion, rubber would be suitable. Finally, the vital statistics. The overall length of a racket must not exceed 27 in. The stringing area must not exceed $8\frac{1}{2}$ in. in length and $7\frac{1}{4}$ in. in breadth.

Ball

This is made of a hollow composition of rubber and butyl. Squash balls comes in three speeds, one of which ("super slow") is specially adapted for use in uncommonly hot climates. Our concern here is with the other two—what are formally known as the "medium" and "slow" balls. The distinction between them is easily explained: use a medium ball in a cold court, and a slow ball in a warm court.

You will play in both kinds of court, but by using the appropriate ball (keep both types in your bag) you defeat the variation in temperature and keep the pace of the game unchanged. If you fool about, it will do you no good. A medium ball in a warm court is too fast. If you use a slow ball on a cold court, you can flog your arm beyond the limits of its strength in trying to maintain a fast pace. Since the major championships happen to be played on warm courts, the slow ball is used. If they were played in cold courts, the medium ball would be used. Yet somehow— in spite of repeated official reminders that the speed of ball used should depend on the type of court—the idea has got around that the slow ball is "king". Don't fall into the trap. When the slow ball is used on a cold court it does your game (in addition to your arm) a lot of harm. For one thing it flatters you—without any real effort or ability you can make the ball die or perform all kinds of angled trickery. The day of reckoning comes when you move to a warm court and find that your control over the ball has deserted you. No longer can you make a kill or play to a good length: the rallies go on and on, while you hit and hit, hoping you can last longer than the other chap. Squash becomes a test of endurance—you lose all the fun and enjoyment of outwitting your opponent by working him out of position and then making a winner. So always pick a ball to suit the court: if in doubt, ask someone who knows the court better than you do. Whatever ball you use, remember that it will get faster when warmed by play (or by the high temperature of some courts). This means that the ball's behaviour at the beginning of the knock-up is no guide to how it will play later. The search for a perfect squash ball has caused—and is still causing—much research, experiment, and frustration. The Australian ball differs slightly from the British in composition and bounce, though both makes come in three speeds. The quest for improvement and compromise is a continuing headache for the game's administrators and

B

the manufacturers. From the players' point of view, the important thing is to use your wits and adapt your game to changes in climate, court, and ball—just as tennis players are always having to adjust their games to the special demands of grass courts, hard courts, and wood. One last note on the ball: it must have an outside diameter of $1\frac{9}{16}$ in. to $1\frac{5}{8}$ in., weigh 360 to 380 grains Apothecaries' or Troy weight (which is not much), and have a matt finish.

Courts

If you have not seen a squash court, imagine a large yet claustrophobic prison cell bounded by high white walls, with the only escape route a flush-fitting door merging into the back wall. Or imagine a pit—constructed above ground level instead of below it. To enjoy the full flavour of the setting, add the fact that squash is the only popular "racket" or "court" game in which both players are on the same side of the "net"—which in squash consists of what is known as the tin, or board (you lose a rally every time you play a shot that is not, as it were, "above board"). The close proximity of two fast-moving players, swinging rackets, underlines the importance of keeping out of each other's way. The diagram gives you a more detailed idea of the court's appearance and dimensions.

Now for a few notes on the various boundaries of the court, starting at the top. When you step onto a strange court, take a good look at the height of the roof and the arrangement of the various fittings beneath it. If you absorb the lessons you read there, there can be no excuse for indiscreet use—or neglect—of the lob. There is no standard height for the roof, and no standard colour. A low roof means that you would be a fool to rely on tactical use of the lob; a high roof gives you more scope. As for colours, there are some courts with dark roofs, which make the flight of the ball difficult to follow up there. Given a high, dark roof, you can cause your opponent a lot of trouble by lobbing. The position of the lighting fixtures and any beams or girders will also (if you are the wise and witty chap we think you are) affect your use of the lob. Lighting systems vary. The traditional arrangement consists of six lamps, three

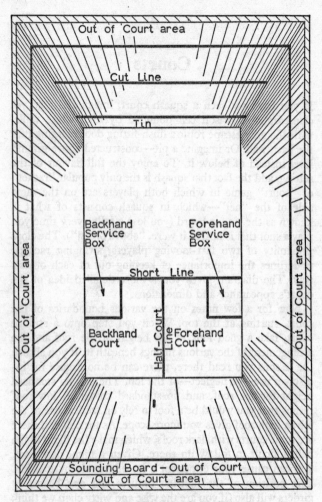

Figure 1 The court from above.

on either side of the court, the two front lamps having reflectors to direct the light onto the front wall. Nowadays there is a move towards fluorescent strip lighting. This has aroused mixed feelings because the "cold" white light it provides differs in quality from that supplied by the traditional lamps. But fluorescent lighting, more expensive to install but cheaper to run, is gradually becoming accepted. Outside courts (as distinct from those tucked away in larger buildings) have glass roofs, so you can play by daylight. If the various fixtures in the roof are unusual, ask if the club have any "local rules" governing match play. What we are saying in all these notes about the roof is simply this: adapt your game to the court.

The plastered walls are usually white or off-white—occasionally apple green, which is restful for the eyes. The walls are affected by humidity, and a sudden change in temperature can make them sweat. In these conditions the geometry of the game goes haywire, because the ball skids off the walls instead of rebounding at the usual angles. When you notice condensation, hit low and hard, and forget about the clever stuff. A sweating court tends to make the floor slippery, too, so that your footwork, like your strokes, has to be more inhibited than usual. As for the door, this is made of thick teak to give the ball the same rebound as the walls. The tin stretching across the bottom of the front wall is made of a resounding material, such as zinc. The play line at the top of the tin protrudes from the wall and is sometimes angled, to deflect the flight of any shot that hits it (this can sometimes help the marker to decide whether the shot was "up" or "down").

The best floors are laid like the floor of a dance hall—that is to say, sprung. This eliminates jarring, helps the player to move about, and, in general, saves the feet some wear and tear. Canadian maple is often used because of its hardness and its light colour (you could not follow the flight of the ball across a dark floor).

In adapting your tactics to the court, the most influential factor is temperature. A warm court means a faster game, with lots of bounce in the ball and the emphasis on concentration, stamina, and accuracy. The rallies are long. The stroke player is at a disadvantage. Indoor courts (i.e., courts constructed as part of a larger building, as in the West End social clubs) are warm—very warm if they happen to be close to a heated swimming pool, or to kitchens. Most of the big championships are played on courts like this, so that players from the provinces (where most of the courts are cold) start with the tactical handicap of having to play a type of game to which they are not accustomed. On cold courts the ball does not bounce much. It travels more slowly and dies more quickly. In these conditions the stroke player can show us all his tricks. Courts that stand out in the open (i.e. courts that are *not* part of a larger, sheltering building that will keep them warm) are usually cold. Right from the start you should learn to recognize—and exploit—the difference between hot and cold courts.

The Language of the Game

Any instructional book falls short of its aims if the terms used are not fully explained. This is particularly relevant to a book on squash, which has a vocabulary appropriate to the game's unique and abundant pleasures. The glossary given here is as comprehensive as we can make it, with two reservations: first, we have not included the words for describing the various parts of the court (since these were given with the diagram on page 24); and second, we give here only the briefest definitions of words explained in detail elsewhere in the book ("lob", "volley", and so on). What it amounts to is that by consulting this glossary, and the diagram on page 24, you can quickly solve any difficulty the language of the game may cause you. That language is itself fascinating. You will soon master it, and the experience will put you, as it were, three points up—(1) You will know more about the game; (2) You will know what you are talking about; and (3) When you discuss the game, or play it, with someone less well versed in the grammar of squash, you will be able to blind him with science! After all, psychological warfare is all part of the fun of the game.

Ace—Term sometimes used to describe an outright service winner—that is, a service which the receiver is unable to return.

Angle—This is an attacking shot played onto the side wall the striker is facing. The ball then ricochets from the side wall to the front wall. The shot can be used for two purposes—one, to get your opponent out of position; two, to make a winner if he is already out of position. Angles can

27

also be referred to as "good lengths" if they die (*see* **Die**)
before rebounding from the opposite side wall. *See*
chapter on Angle. **Reverse angle**—A similar shot, but
played across court—onto the wall to which the striker
has his back turned. For example, if the striker plays a
backhand stroke, hitting the ball onto the right-hand side
wall, this is a reverse angle. *See* chapter on Reverse
Angle.

Appeal—A player may appeal against the marker's decision, which may then be reconsidered by the referee—
or by the marker himself if he is in sole charge of the
match. *See* chapter on Rules.

Backhand—A stroke played on the striker's left-hand side,
the head of the racket moving from the vicinity of the left
shoulder and following through beyond the right shoulder.
Backhand court—The left-hand side of the court.

Back-wall boast—*See* **Boast**.

Boast—A defensive stroke forced upon a player when the
ball is returned to such an awkward position (by a good
length shot to a back corner) that usually he can only
make a return by first playing the ball onto a side wall
or the back wall. **Back-wall boast**—A boast off the back
wall (the word "boast" alone is normally taken to refer
to a side-wall boast). **Double boast**—In this case the
ball hits both side walls (or the back wall and one side
wall) before striking the front wall. For all types of boast,
see chapter on Boast.

Check—Many players try to keep up a pretty fast pace,
with the aim of beating an opponent by speed. But by
checking the stroke immediately before hitting the ball,
the striker can unexpectedly slow down his return. This
sudden variation in pace can catch the opponent flat-
footed, or make him mistime his stroke by striking too
soon.

Clinger—A shot that travels straight back down the nearest
side wall and clings to it. Basically a negative shot, but

tactically useful, since it is difficult to return and cannot be attacked. In returning it, do not take a full swing: be satisfied to scrape the ball carefully off the wall with a relaxed grip, letting the wrist do the work.

Crowding—A player is said to be crowding his opponent when he stands or moves so close that the opponent's freedom of stroke or movement is restricted.

Cut—This is severe back-spin (similar in effect to "chop" in table tennis), which is applied to the ball in order to bring it down sharply as soon as it has hit the front wall.

Cut service—The application of cut when serving, to bring the ball down steeply on a good length, or to attempt a nick. *See* **Nick.**

Dead nick—*See* **Nick.**

Die—The ball is said to die when it loses all its impetus and trickles so close to the floor and a wall that it cannot be returned. This is usually achieved by directing the ball into the nick, or very close to it, after applying cut or slice to the stroke.

Double boast—*See* **Boast.**

Drop shot—Usually played from the front of the court, this is a gently hit stroke, with cut, intended to die in the nick close to one of the front corners. *See* chapter on Drop Shot.

Drop-volley—*See* **Volley.**

Fair view—Immediately a shot is played, the man who played it must get out of the way in order to allow his opponent a fair view of the ball and freedom of stroke. The opponent must be free to move in a straight line towards the ball, without obstruction. *See* chapter on Rules.

Fault—A service that contravenes the Rules. **Foot fault**— Occurs if the server, in the act of striking the ball, has not got at least one foot on the floor and within (not touching) the lines marking the service box. For all faults, *see* chapter on Rules.

Follow-through—In squash, as in most ball games, an important part of every stroke occurs *after* impact. The completion of the swing is called the follow-through.

Foot fault—*See* **Fault.**

Forehand—Stroke played on the striker's right-hand side, the head of the racket moving from the vicinity of the right shoulder and following through beyond the left shoulder. **Forehand court**—The right-hand side of the court.

Gallery—Accommodation for spectators, providing a view over the back wall and, on some championship courts, over the side walls. The gallery of a squash court provides a similar view—though much closer to the action—to the gallery of a theatre.

Game—The first player to win nine points wins a game, except that on the first call of "eight-all" hand-out (*see* **Hand**) may, if he chooses, set the game to two: this means that the first player to score two more points wins the game. *See* **Match, Set,** and chapter on Rules.

Game ball—When the server (hand-in) needs one point to win the game. There is no call of "match point" in squash: when a match reaches this stage, the call is still "game ball".

Half-volley—Stroke played neither before nor after the bounce, but while the ball is still in contact with the floor. *See* chapter on Half-volley.

Hand—The period of play from the time a player becomes server until he becomes receiver (thus several points may be scored in one hand). **Hand-in**—The player who is serving. **Hand-out**—The player who is receiving service. (The marker also calls "hand-out" when the server loses a rally.)

Kill—A heavily cut stroke that "kills" the ball and makes it impossible to retrieve. Kills are usually achieved by hard hits into the nick of the nearest side wall (though cross-court kills are both spectacular and satisfying). At the highest level some players hit the ball so hard that they can occasionally kill it without using the nick. What happens here is that a powerful and well timed shot takes all the resilience out of the soft ball so that, as if punctured, it dies on leaving the front wall.

Knock-up—A period of five minutes, before a match, in which players are allowed to practice on court. *See* chapter on Match Play.

Length—This describes a stroke that hits the ball straight up and down a side wall—or across court—at such a pace that the ball dies in a back corner after the first bounce. It may fail to reach the back wall, or may reach it only to drop sharply and die, instead of rebounding. *See* chapter on Length.

Let—An undecided rally, which is played again. Common causes of lets are: a doubtful return; the denial of a fair view; a player hit by the ball or a racket; a player's inability to play a proper stroke because his opponent is crowding him; and obstruction of the striker as he tries to get to the ball. *See* chapter on Rules.

Lob—A stroke that sends the ball soaring over the opponent to drop into the back of the court. **Lob service**—The lob used as a service. *See* chapter on Lob.

Marker—An official (usually a professional) appointed to control a match and call the score. If no referee is appointed, the marker exercises the referee's powers as well as his own.

Masking—A technique vital to successful tactics, since it is the basis of deception. A player can mask his intentions by a sudden turn of the wrist just before impact, thus playing a drop shot or angle when a good length is expected, or vice versa. The opponent is caught on the wrong foot or persuaded to move the wrong way. The Egyptians, who have particularly good wrists, are adept at masking. *See* chapter on Match Play.

Match—Consists of the best of three or five games

(championship matches are decided by the best of five games).

Nick—The junction of walls and floor. Also describes a shot that goes into the nick and therefore bounces unpredictably (this shot is sometimes called a half-nick). **Dead nick**—This occurs when the ball lands full in the nick and, instead of bouncing, rolls along the floor and is therefore unplayable. Obviously a useful shot to play, though it demands great accuracy—or luck!

No set—*See* Set.

Not up—Called by the marker when the ball is struck on its second bounce, or when the ball is not returned above the board in accordance with the rules. The striker loses the rally.

Opening up the court—Tactical process of playing a stroke that forces the opponent into a corner, so that almost the entire court is left open for a winner.

Out of court—Called by the marker when the ball touches any part of the walls outside the playing area, or touches or passes over any beams, girders, or lights in the roof of the court. The lines marking the upper limits of the playing area are themselves out of court.

Penalty point—Usually awarded only at the game's higher levels; this is a more severe penalty than a let. It means that—instead of replaying the rally, as in the case of a let—the offending player loses the hand (if he is hand-in) or loses a point (if he is hand-out). A common cause for the award of a penalty point: when a player fails to give his opponent a fair view of the ball and freedom of stroke. *See* chapter on Rules.

Play—Called by the marker if a service is good, if a fault is played by the receiver, or if the marker considers a rally should continue in spite of a doubtful stroke.

Pull—When positioned for a normal forehand or backhand drive, a player may fox his opponent with a pull. Instead of playing straight, and hitting the ball when it is alongside him, the striker takes the ball in advance, slightly in front of him. This puts the striker's body between the ball and his opponent, who is temporarily unsighted, and it also means that the ball is hit across court, instead of up and down the nearest side wall as the receiver expects. The stroke begins farther than usual from the shoulder of the racket arm. Its aim is to catch the opponent on the wrong foot or make him move the wrong way.

Put out—A player who is hand-in is said to be "put out" when he loses a rally.

Rally—The continuous exchange of shots between the service and the moment when hand-in either scores a point or becomes hand-out.

Receiver—At the beginning of a rally, hand-out is the receiver. Afterwards, "receiver" denotes the player who has to make the next stroke but one.

Referee—An additional official, usually an amateur, who is appointed at important championships to assist the marker and adjudicate on tricky decisions. The referee awards lets or penalty points. A player may appeal to the referee to reconsider decisions made by the marker. The referee deals with all appeals. *See* **Appeal.**

Reverse angle—*See* **Angle.**

Set—It is part of the marker's job to remind hand-out that the score is 8-all and that hand-out must make a choice before the next service. Hand-out may decide to play the best of three points ("set two") or ask for "no set" (often called "sudden death"), which means that the player winning the next point (not necessarily the next rally) wins the game. The usual choice is "set two"— which hand-out may indicate to the marker by raising two fingers (a spectacle that sometimes shocks spectators who have never seen squash before!) So a game cannot go farther than 10-9.

Side-wall boast—*See* **Boast.**

Side-wall smash—*See* **Smash.**

Slice—A stroke that (in the case of a forehand) puts clockwise spin on the ball. A sliced backhand makes the ball spin anti-clockwise. In each case, the arc of the swing and the position of the racket head differ from the normal stroke. The effect is to make the ball shoot away from the striker at a much greater angle than usual. *See* chapter on Spin.

Smash—A full-blooded volley, played with the head of the racket above shoulder height. If you can make the ball rebound from the front wall into the nick, your opponent will be confounded by the angle of the shot as well as its speed. He may even be beaten by an outright kill. But in squash, as in tennis, a genuine smash can only be played safely from the front half of the court. **Side-wall smash**—Played onto the side wall, this is really a violent version of the angle (*see* **Angle**). *See* chapter on Volley.

Striker—The player whose turn it is to hit the ball.

Sudden death—*See* **Set.**

Time—Called by the marker (as by a barman!) when he wishes to stop play. The marker also calls "Time" after the five minutes allowed for the knock-up; and after the permitted interval between games (usually one minute, but two minutes between the fourth and fifth games if the match goes that far).

Turning—This usually occurs when the ball (especially from a service) rebounds so awkwardly from side wall to back wall that it cannot be returned in the conventional way. So the striker turns round anti-clockwise in the backhand corner, following the ball, in order to play a forehand stroke—or turns round clockwise in the forehand corner, in order to play a backhand. *See* chapter on Etiquette.

Volley—Stroke played before the ball has bounced. *See* chapter on Volley. **Drop-volley**—Drop shot played before the ball has bounced. *See* chapters on Drop shot and Volley.

The Rules of Squash Rackets

THE SINGLES GAME

(As adopted by the International Squash Rackets Federation, January 1967)

1. THE GAME, HOW PLAYED. The game of squash rackets is played between two players with standard rackets, with balls bearing the standard mark of the S.R.A. and in a rectangular court of standard dimensions enclosed on all four sides.

2. THE SCORE. A match shall consist of the best of three or five games at the option of the promoters of the competition. Each game is 9 up: that is to say the player who first wins 9 points wins the game except that, on the score being called 8-all for the first time, hand-out may, if he chooses, before the next service is delivered, set the game to 2, in which case the player who first scores two more points wins the game. Hand-out must in either case clearly indicate his choice to the marker, if any, and to his opponent.

— NOTE TO REFEREES —

If hand-out does not make clear his choice before the next service, the referee shall stop play and require him to do so.

3. POINTS, HOW SCORED. Points can only be scored by hand-in. When a player fails to serve or to make a good return in accordance with the rules, his opponent wins the stroke. When hand-in wins a stroke, he scores a point; when hand-out wins a stroke, he becomes hand-in.

4. THE RIGHT TO SERVE. The right to serve first is decided by the spin of a racket. Thereafter the server continues to serve until he loses a stroke, when his opponent becomes the server, and so on throughout the match.

5. SERVICE. The ball before being struck shall be thrown in the air and shall not touch the walls or floor. The ball shall be served on to the front wall so that on its return, unless volleyed, it would fall to the floor in the quarter court nearest the back wall and opposite to the server's box from which the service has been delivered.

At the beginning of each game and of each hand, the server may serve from either box, but after scoring a point he shall then serve from the other and so on alternately as long as he remains hand-in or until the end of the game. If the server serves from the wrong box there shall be no penalty and the service shall count as if served from the right box, except that hand-out may, if he does not attempt to take the service, demand that it be served from the other box.

6. GOOD SERVICE. A service is good which is not a fault or which does not result in the server serving his hand out in accordance with rule 9. If the server serves one fault he shall serve again.

7. FAULT. A service is a fault (unless the server serves his hand out under rule 9):

    (a) If the server fails to stand with one foot at least within and not touching the line surrounding the service box (called a foot fault);

    (b) If the ball is served onto or below the cut line;

    (c) If the ball served first touches the floor on or in front of the short line;

    (d) If the ball served first touches the floor in the wrong half court or on the half-court line.

        (The wrong half court is the left for a service from the left-hand box and the right for a service from the right-hand box.)

8. FAULT, IF TAKEN. Hand-out may take a fault. If he attempts to do so, the service thereupon becomes good and the ball continues in play. If he does not attempt to do so, the ball shall cease to be in play provided that, if the ball, before it has bounced twice upon the floor, touches the server or anything he wears or carries, the server shall lose the stroke.

9. SERVING HAND-OUT. The server serves his hand out and loses the stroke:

(a) If the ball is served onto or below the board or out of court or against any part of the court before the front wall;

(b) If he fails to strike the ball or strikes the ball more than once;

(c) If he serves two consecutive faults;

(d) If the ball before it has bounced twice upon the floor, or has been struck by his opponent touches the server or anything he wears or carries.

10. LET. A let is an undecided stroke and the service or rally in respect of which a let is allowed shall not count and the server shall serve again from the same box. A let shall not annul a previous fault.

11. THE PLAY. After a good service has been delivered the players return the ball alternately until one or other fails to make a good return or the ball otherwise ceases to be in play in accordance with the rules.

12. GOOD RETURN. A return is good if the ball, before it has bounced twice upon the floor, is returned by the striker on to the front wall above the board without touching the floor, or any part of the striker's body or clothing, provided the ball is not hit twice or out of court.

— NOTE TO REFEREES —

It shall not be considered a good return if the ball touches the board either before or after it hits the front wall.

13. **STROKES, HOW WON.** A player wins a stroke:
   (a) Under rule 9;
   (b) If his opponent fails to make a good return of the ball in play;
   (c) If the ball in play touches the striker or his opponent or anything he wears or carries, except as is otherwise provided by rules 14 and 15.

14. **HITTING AN OPPONENT WITH THE BALL.** If an otherwise good return of the ball has been made, but before reaching the front wall it hits the striker's opponent or his racket or anything he wears or carries, then:
   (a) If the ball would have made a good return and would have struck the front wall without first touching any other wall, the striker shall win the stroke, except that, if the striker shall have followed the ball round and so turned before making a stroke, a let shall be allowed;
   (b) If the ball would otherwise have made a good return, a let shall be allowed;
   (c) If the ball would not have made a good return, the striker shall lose the stroke.

The ball shall cease to be in play, even if it subsequently goes up.

15. **FURTHER ATTEMPTS TO HIT THE BALL.** If the striker strikes at and misses the ball, he may make further attempts to return it. If after being missed, the ball accidentally touches his opponent or his racket or anything he wears or carries, then:
   (a) If the striker could otherwise have made a good return, a let shall be allowed;
   (b) If the striker could not have made a good return he loses the stroke.

If any such further attempt is successful but the ball before reaching the front wall hits the striker's opponent or his racket or anything he wears or carries, a let shall be allowed and rule 14 (a) shall not apply.

16. APPEALS. An appeal may be made against any decision of the marker.

    (i) The following rules shall apply to appeals on the service:

        (a) No appeal shall be made in respect of foot faults.

        (b) No appeal shall be made in respect of the marker's call of "fault" to the first service.

        (c) If the marker calls "fault" to the second service, the server may appeal and, if the decision is reversed, a let shall be allowed.

        (d) If the marker calls "play" to the second service, hand-out may appeal even if he attempts to take the ball, and if the decision is reversed hand-in becomes hand-out.

        (e) If the marker calls "play" to the first service, hand-out may appeal if he makes no attempt to take the ball. If the appeal is disallowed hand-out shall lose the stroke.

    (ii) An appeal under rule 12 or 16 (i) (d) shall be made at the end of the rally in which the stroke in dispute has been played.

    (iii) In all cases where an appeal for a let is desired, the appeal shall be made by addressing to the referee or marker the words "Let, please". Play shall thereupon cease until the referee or marker has given his decision.

    (iv) No appeal may be made after the delivery of a service for anything that occurred before that service was delivered.

17. FAIR VIEW AND FREEDOM OF STROKE.

    (a) After making a stroke a player must get out of his opponent's way as much as possible.

    If, in the opinion of the referee, a player has not made every effort to do this the referee shall stop play and award a stroke to his opponent.

(b) When a player:
　(i) fails to give his opponent a fair view of the ball,

　　(Note: a player shall be considered to have had a fair view unless the ball returns too close to his opponent for the player to sight it adequately for the purpose of making a stroke;)

　(ii) fails to avoid interfering with, or crowding his opponent in getting to or striking at the ball,

　(iii) fails to allow his opponent, as far as his opponent's position allows him, freedom to play the ball to any part of the front wall and to either side wall near the front wall; the referee may on appeal or without waiting for an appeal allow a let; but if in the opinion of the referee a player has not made every effort to comply with these requirements of the rule, the referee shall stop play and award a stroke to his opponent.

Notwithstanding anything contained above, if a player suffers interference from or distraction by his opponent, and in the opinion of the referee is thus prevented from making a winning return, he shall be awarded the stroke.

— NOTE TO REFEREES —

(a) The practice of impeding an opponent's strokes by crowding or by obscuring his view is highly detrimental to the game and referees should have no hesitation in enforcing the penultimate paragraph of this rule.

(b) The words "interfering with . . . his opponent in getting to . . . the ball" must be interpreted so as to include the case of a player having to wait for an excessive swing of his opponent's racket.

18. **LET, WHEN ALLOWED.** Notwithstanding anything contained in these rules.

    (i) A let may be allowed:

        (a) If, owing to the position of the striker, his opponent is unable to avoid being touched by the ball before the return is made;

— NOTE TO REFEREES —

This rule shall be construed to include the cases of the striker whose position in front of his opponent makes it impossible for the latter to see the ball or who shapes as if to play the ball and changes his mind at the last moment preferring to take the ball off the back wall, the ball in either case hitting the opponent who is between the striker and the back wall. This is not, however, to be taken as conflicting in any way with the referee's duties under rule 17.

        (b) If the ball in play touches any article lying in the court;

        (c) If the player refrains from hitting the ball owing to a reasonable fear of injuring his opponent;

        (d) If the player in the act of striking touches his opponent;

        (e) If the referee is asked to decide an appeal and is unable to do so;

        (f) If the player drops his racket, calls out or in any other way distracts the attention of his opponent and the referee considers such occurrence to have caused his opponent to lose the stroke.

    (ii) A let shall be allowed:

        (a) If hand-out is not ready and does not attempt to take the service;

        (b) If a ball breaks during play;

        (c) If an otherwise good return has been made,

but the ball goes out of court on its first
bounce.

(d) As provided for by rules 14, 15, 16 (i) (c) and
22.

(iii) Provided always that no let shall be allowed:

(a) In respect of any stroke which a player
attempts to make, unless in making the stroke
he touches his opponent; except as provided
for under rules 18 (ii) (b) and (c) and 15.

(b) Unless the striker could have made a good
return.

(iv) Unless an appeal is made by one of the players, no
let shall be allowed except where these rules
definitely provide for a let, namely rules 14 (a),
14 (b) and 17 and paragraphs (ii) (b) and (c) of
rule 18.

19.   NEW BALL. At any time when the ball is not in
actual play a new ball may be substituted by mutual consent
of the players or an appeal by either player at the discretion
of the referee.

20.   KNOCK-UP. The referee shall allow to either player
or to the two players together a period of five minutes
during the hour preceding the start of a match for knocking
up in a court in which a match is to be played. The choice
of knocking up first shall be decided by the spin of a racket.

21.   PLAY IN A MATCH IS TO BE CONTINUOUS.
After the first service is delivered, play shall be continuous
so far as is practical, provided that at any time play may be
suspended owing to bad light or other circumstances beyond
the control of the players for such period as the referee shall
decide. The referee shall award the match to the opponent
of any player who, in his opinion, persists, after due warning,
in delaying the play in order to recover his strength or wind,
or for any other reason. However, an interval of one minute
shall be permitted between games and of two minutes between the fourth and fifth games of a five-games match. A

player may leave the court during such intervals, but shall be ready to resume play at the end of the stated time. Should he fail to do so when required by the referee the match shall be awarded to his opponent. In the event of play being suspended for the day, the match shall start afresh, unless both players agree to the contrary.

— NOTE TO REFEREES —

A player may not open the door or leave the court other than between games without the referee's permission.

22. DUTIES OF MARKER. The game is controlled by the marker, who shall call the play and the score. The server's score is called first. He shall call "Play" in respect of a good service and "Fault" (rule 7 (b) (c) and (d)), "Foot Fault" (rule 7 (a)), "Out of Court" or "Not up" as the case may be. If in the course of play the marker calls "Not up" or "Out of Court" the rally shall cease. In doubtful cases the marker should always call "Play". If the marker's decision is reversed on appeal a "let" shall be allowed except that if the marker fails to call a ball "Not up" or "Out of Court" and, on appeal, it is ruled that such was in fact the case, the stroke shall be awarded accordingly.

If after the server has served one fault a "let" is allowed, the marker shall call "One fault" before the server serves again.

When no referee is appointed, the marker shall exercise all the powers of the referee.

23. THE REFEREE. A referee may be appointed, to whom all appeals shall be directed, including appeals from the marker's decisions and calls. He shall in no way interfere with the marker's counting of the game except upon appeal by one of the players or as provided for in rule 17. The referee shall decide all appeals. The decision of the referee shall be final.

— FIRST NOTE TO REFEREES —

Notwithstanding the above, in the absence of an appeal, if it is evident that the score has been called incorrectly, the referee shall draw the marker's attention to this fact.

— SECOND NOTE TO REFEREES —

It is recommended that, when there are both a referee and a marker, the referee shall appoint the marker to call foot faults and the referee shall indicate, if necessary, the box from which hand-in shall serve.

24. POWER OF REFEREE IN EXCEPTIONAL CASES. The referee has power to order:

    (a) A player who has left the court to play on;

    (b) A player to leave the court for any reason whatsoever and to award the match to his opponent;

    (c) A match to be awarded to a player whose opponent fails to be present in the court within ten minutes of the advertised time of play.

    (d) Play to be stopped in order that a player or players may be warned that their conduct on the court is leading to an infringement of the rules.

— NOTE TO REFEREES —

A referee should avail himself of this rule as early as possible where one or other of the players is showing a tendency to break the provisions of rule 17.

APPENDIX I

DEFINITIONS

Board. The expression denoting a line, the top edge of which is 19 inches from the floor, set out upon the upper edge of a band of resonant material fixed upon the front wall and extending the full width of the court.

Cut Line. A line set out upon the front wall, six feet above the floor and extending the full width of the court.

Game Ball. The state of the game when the server requires one point to win is said to be "Game Ball".

Half-Court Line. A line set out upon the floor parallel to the side walls, dividing the back half of the court into two equal parts called right half court and left half court respectively.

Hand-in. The player who serves.

Hand-out. The player who receives the service.

Hand. The period from the time when a player becomes hand-in until he becomes hand-out.

Not-up. The expression used to denote that a ball has not been returned above the board in accordance with the rules.

Out of Court. The ball is out of court when it touches the front, sides or back of the court above the area prepared for play or passes over any cross bars or other part of the roof of the court. The lines delimiting such area, the lighting equipment and the roof are out of court.

Service Box or Box. A delimited area in each half court from within which hand-in serves.

Short Line. A line set out upon the floor parallel to and 18 feet from the front wall and extending the full width of the court.

Striker. The player whose turn it is to play after the ball has hit the front wall.

APPENDIX II

STANDARD DIMENSIONS OF A SINGLES COURT

Length 32 feet	Breadth 21 feet
Height to upper edge of cut line on front wall	6 feet
Height to lower edge of front-wall line .	15 feet

Height to lower edge of back-wall line .   .   7 feet

Distance to further edge of short line from front
wall   .   .   .   .   18 feet

Height to upper edge of board from ground .   19 inches

Thickness of board (flat or rounded at top) $\frac{1}{2}$ to 1 inch

Height of side-wall line: The diagonal line joining the
front-wall line and the back-wall line.

The service boxes shall be entirely enclosed on three sides
within the court by lines, the short line forming the side
nearest to the front wall, the side wall bounding the fourth
side.

The internal dimensions of the service boxes shall be
5 ft. 3 in.

All dimensions in the court shall be measured, where
practicable, from the junction of the floor and front wall.

The lines marking the boundaries of the court shall be
2 inches in width.

In respect of the outer boundary lines on the walls, it is
suggested that the plaster should be so shaped as to produce
a concave channel along such lines.

The width of other painted lines shall not exceed 2 inches.

All walls shall be white or near white. The space below
the board shall be white. All lines shall be coloured red.

The front wall shall be of composition. The side walls and
back wall shall be of wood or of composition.

The floor should be of wood for covered courts and of
composition for open courts.

The board and the space below it to the floor and the area
above the height of play on the back wall should be constructed of some resonant material.

APPENDIX III

DIMENSIONS OF A RACKET

The overall length shall not exceed 27 inches. The internal stringing area shall not exceed 8$\frac{1}{2}$ inches in length by

$7\frac{1}{4}$ inches in breadth, and the framework of the head shall measure not more than $\frac{9}{16}$ inch across the face by $\frac{13}{16}$ inch deep.

The framework of the head shall be of wood. The handle shaft shall be made of wood, cane, metal or glass fibre. The grip and foundation may be made of any suitable material.

APPENDIX IV

SPECIFICATION FOR STANDARD SQUASH RACKETS BALLS

1. Balls must pass the testing committee of the S.R.A. as being satisfactory in play.
2. Size: Outside diameter $1\frac{9}{16}$ to $1\frac{10}{16}$ inches.
3. Weight: 360 to 380 grains (Apothecaries' or Troy weight).
4. Balls must have a matt finish.

The Grip

When you come to think about it, the way you grip the racket is the basis of all your game's virtues—or all its vices. With the right grip, you can master each of the game's techniques in turn. With a faulty grip every difficulty is exaggerated and some may be insuperable. True, there can be small variations to suit the individual, particularly to suit the size and strength of the fingers and wrist. But the basic grip is the same, and everything depends on it. If you get used to treating the racket as a hammer, it will be a difficult business changing to the correct grip later on—as you will have to, if you are going to improve. So start off on the right foot, or in this case, the right grip. If you can check it with a professional, so much the better: he will spot a flaw instantly.

There is a simple method of finding the right grip. Open the hand, with the palm upwards, and slightly spread the fingers. With the head of the racket horizontal, put the handle into the palm of your hand, so that the butt rests on the heel of the hand and slants across the palm between the thumb and forefinger. Now grip the handle by closing round it the second, third, and fourth fingers. Curl the forefinger round the handle, too, but slightly away from the other fingers, so that it will stretch farther along the handle. The thumb curls round the handle as if to join the forefinger, but does not touch it. Do not let the thumb lie uselessly *along* the handle—it must curl *round* the handle. Now examine the grip and let us see how it works. The tip of the little finger should be at least ¾ in. from the end of the handle. The three fingers (second, third, and fourth) tucked

48

in together give you a firm grip and allow your wrist freedom of movement. The thumb and forefinger guide and control the racket so that you can place the ball accurately, and also act as support when you hit hard, or volley.

The grip is the same for backhand and forehand, though the position of the wrist is obviously different because you

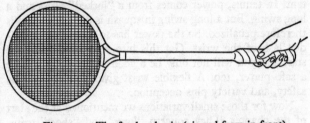

Figure 2   The forehand grip (viewed from in front).

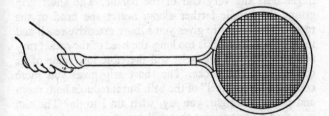

Figure 3   The backhand grip (viewed from in front).

have to keep the face of the racket "open" (that is, slanted so that the top edge of the racket is behind the bottom edge). On the forehand this means that the back of your hand faces to your right. On the forehand you turn the wrist so that the back of your hand faces upwards. But the grip itself does not change. Only the wrist. Squash is such a fast game that you have no time to adjust your grip. If you do adjust it, you're in trouble: for one thing, the ball comes to you so quickly that changing the grip invites technical errors; for another, your concentration will be momentarily diverted from the ball. Once you start messing about like this, you will throw points away or keep on apologizing for hitting lucky returns off the wood.

One of the basic principles of a good grip is that it allows complete freedom for using the wrist. This is very important. In tennis, power comes from a "locked" wrist and a long swing. But a long swing in squash is dangerous and is therefore penalized. So the power has to come from a sudden lash of the wrist. Get this into your head from the start and you will not only be a good player—you will be a safe player, too. A flexible wrist gives you power plus safety, and variety plus deception.

Now for those small variations we mentioned at the start of the chapter. They concern "long" and "short" grips. The long grip—the one we have taught you—has the little finger near the very end of the handle. The short grip grasps the handle farther along, nearer the head of the racket. The long grip gives you a more extensive reach and more power. But if it is too long, the head of the racket may feel unwieldy and the wrist will therefore lose some of its control over the stroke. The short grip gives you more control, a better "feel" of the ball. But it reduces both reach and power. All right, you say, what am I to do? The aim is to find a compromise that will suit the size and strength of your wrist and fingers. Try a long grip first. Then experiment a bit to find the position that feels most comfortable. Remember that control over the ball is vital. If you have a small hand and a weak wrist, a shorter grip might be best— but don't overdo it at the expense of your reach. Finally, having found the position that suits you, cultivate it and stick to it. This position (like the actual arrangement of fingers and thumb) should never be adjusted during the course of a rally.

Footwork

The thing about footwork in squash is that in a confined area you have five moving bodies—two players, two rackets, and a ball. All these (especially the ball) are carving their way through the air at all sorts of speeds and angles. Your job is to make your opponent hurtle about like a madman while you keep out of his way and get into position to play your own strokes. In these circumstances the cricket professional's advice to young batsmen ("Find the ball. Go there. Hit it.") is hardly sufficient for our purpose. We shall discuss footwork more fully in dealing with each stroke, but meantime there are a few important general principles you should master. These mostly spring from the prime need for speed—off the mark, and in turning. ("Basic" speed—for example, the ability to run 100 yards quickly—is not essential.) In acquiring the necessary agility you have to "dance" rather than run; to take more short steps than big strides; to glide rather than bound. Keep your feet reasonably close together, because this will make it easier for you to turn quickly, neatly, and in balance, instead of lunging awkwardly. During a rally your knees should always be slightly bent, your weight slightly forward and on the balls or toes of your feet, not the heels. And you should keep moving—this is less exhausting than "stop-go" methods. While the ball is buzzing about you will never have time to stand still, because after every shot you play there are two urgent jobs to do: getting back to the centre of the court so that you are in position and facing the front wall, and keeping your eyes on the ball.

There is a perfect position for every stroke—a perfect

place to go, a perfectly balanced arrangement of feet, body, arms, and racket. Always aim for this perfection. You will not always have time to achieve it, but the harder you try, the more chance you will have of playing the stroke you want to play. You can play off the "wrong" foot deliberately, to confuse your opponent, but this is advanced stuff—learn how to do things right before you experiment with doing them wrong. (The most successful crooks always know the law inside out!) To sum up, remember that to play a controlled stroke you have to be properly balanced; that to be properly balanced you have to be in position with time to spare; that to be in position with time to spare, you need anticipation (watch that ball) and speed off the mark. Work on it—and in time you will cover the court with flowing ease and instinctive assurance.

Forehand

The forehand is a natural stroke and should not be complicated by too much theory. All we are trying to do here is to help you play it with maximum efficiency on a squash court. This is merely a question of arranging yourself, and your racket, in the most balanced and effective way—in relation, of course, to the position of the ball. Regard these notes as snippets of good advice, rather than a routine to be learnt parrot fashion. Perhaps the best way to set about it is to split the stroke into its three separate components—preparation, impact, and follow-through. Remember that you are playing a simple, straightforward stroke. The ball is coming down the right-hand (forehand) side wall. You want to intercept the ball at the moment when an imaginary line between your left foot, the ball, and the side wall will form a right-angle with that wall. Your aim is to smack the ball hard and low onto the front wall so that it will come back straight and low down the side wall to a good length. Here we go then . . .

Preparation

Turn to face the side wall and put your left foot forward, parallel with the front wall. Knee slightly bent. Toes pointing straight at the side wall. As the ball approaches and that left foot goes firmly down, with your weight on it, two other things should happen—left shoulder down (over the left foot) and racket back and up in a line parallel with the side wall. Elbow bent. The head of the racket (higher than the right shoulder) is not in line with the forearm, because the wrist is bent upwards and backwards—"cocked". By doing this you will get maximum "whip" on your shot (hitting a squash ball is rather like whipping a top, if you can remember how that was done!). Get down to it. Tuck your stomach in. Right . . . You are properly poised, like a tiger ready to pounce on his lunch . . . You are watching the ball every inch of the way.

Impact

Don't let the ball pass you before impact. The ideal spot for the explosion is about 9 in. from the floor and about 2 ft. from the left foot, bang in line between left shoulder, left foot, and side wall. Lean into the shot. Swing low, but keep the head of the racket up and its face "open" (that is, slightly slanted so that the upper edge of the racket's head is behind the lower edge). The position of the feet—and the arc of the swing in relation to the feet—is not unlike that of a straight drive played off the front foot in cricket. Don't play the stroke too close to the body, or you will be cramped. On impact, your shoulders are parallel with the side wall, your body perfectly balanced and so still that you could be posing for a picture: at that moment, all the action is concentrated in racket, wrist, and arms.

Follow-through

As you hit the ball, the racket follows through, up over the left shoulder (not round it, which would put you off balance and endanger your opponent) in line with the path of the ball. Your forearm finishes close to the body, your hand just below the left shoulder. You have hit a superb shot. But you do not stand there and admire it. Immediately after impact you are already "pushing off" to hurry back to the middle of the court. You are still watching the ball. You are ready to give your next demonstration of perfect stroke play: preparation, impact, and follow-through.

But we will assume that, on occasion, you share with

every other human being the capacity for error. The important thing is to be constructive in your exasperation, to work out why you made the mistake. Here are a few clues to help your investigations. *You hit down?* Well, perhaps you were late in your preparations, in getting the racket back. Perhaps you failed to keep the face of the racket "open". *Maybe you hit the ball too high.* This could happen because you struck the ball too soon—while the racket was rising, towards the end of the swing. Or because your weight was on the wrong foot (that is, the back one). *Perhaps your direction was at fault.* Clumsy footwork might be the cause. If you plant your left foot too far across towards the side wall, consider the implications: as the ball rebounds from the front wall it will be heading straight for your left leg, instead of for the gap between left leg and side wall. You cannot let the ball hit you. Nor do you want to play a cramped shot that may leave a dent in your shinbone. So bad footwork forces you to play the ball too soon—while it is between your left leg and the front wall. Your swing will go round the leg instead of parallel with the side wall, and the ball will go across court instead of down the right-hand side wall. Equally, you might send the ball in the wrong direction because you hit it too late, letting it pass you before impact: in this case the ball goes onto the side wall first, instead of the front wall, and finishes in the middle of the court—a sitting duck for a grateful opponent. To avoid these misdirected shots, you must swing on the path you want the ball to follow. To do this, get your feet and body round to face the side wall, with your left foot beside the ball and your left shoulder down, over that left foot, before making contact. And crack the ball while it is between your left foot and the side wall.

All these are specific causes of specific errors. There are a few general points to bear in mind, too. Perhaps you were too close to the ball when you hit it. Perhaps you failed to keep your body still at the moment of impact. Perhaps (most important of all) you took your eye off the ball for a second. The overall lesson is this: think what you're doing, and concentrate.

Backhand

The same general principles apply to forehand and backhand alike, with the obvious proviso that everything happens the other way round—left becomes right, and so on. There are a few points demanding special emphasis when you play a backhand drive. The first is that, as this is a less "natural" stroke than the forehand, it is vital to get "set up" right, to have feet and body properly arranged. The second is that to keep the face of the racket "open" the wrist has to be turned so that, on the backhand, the back of the hand faces upwards (as we explained in the chapter on the grip). The third is that the backswing—the full backswing—must be made in plenty of time (at the moment when your weight comes down on the right foot): a late start may tempt you to snatch at the ball and play a rather wild follow-through, instead of using the orthodox swing. You cannot compensate for a late start. The fourth is the follow-through itself, which, on the backhand, can be highly dangerous. For the ordinary backhand drive, straight down the side wall, follow-through parallel with the side wall, even as the racket starts rising at the end of its swing. The racket should finish almost vertical, between your right shoulder and the front wall. Never swing the follow-through round the body so that the racket finishes pointing to the right-hand side wall. Such a stroke would be (a) technically bad, (b) dangerous, and (c) illegal. In this respect a flexible wrist is blatantly important, because a locked wrist would invite a follow-through fraught with risk.

Make a point of getting your backhand right from the start of your squash career. The wall prevents you from "running round" a weak backhand, as some tennis players do. So you cannot afford weakness on that flank. In general, you should use it for all the shots you play on the left-hand side of the court, just as on the right-hand side you should use your forehand.

The clues we gave about rectifying mistakes on the forehand apply to the backhand, too. Remember the advice we have just given about keeping the face of the racket "open", about the importance of the backswing and follow-through. Most of all, remember that more often than not a bad backhand is due to bad footwork. You must get that right foot across, so that at the moment of impact the right foot is nearer than the left foot to the side wall. Your body has to be turned to the left in good time, so that your right shoulder comes down over your right foot before you hit the ball.

Length

Competitive games are meaningless unless you play to win. In squash, as in tennis, there are three ways of doing this: hitting outright winners; forcing your opponent to make mistakes; or a combination of the two. In every case the basis of a winning game is the same—the ability to put your opponent on the defensive by hitting to a good length. You can hit hard or you can hit gently. You can hit straight up and down the nearest side wall, or you can hit across court. But if you go for a length with a *gently* hit cross-court stroke, this must obviously be a lob—or your opponent will intercept it. When we talk about length, we are primarily discussing a hard hit ball that dies in one of the back corners after the first bounce—or is so close to death that the opponent has the devil of a job digging it out of the corner and making his return. If you strike a length, your opponent is continually in two minds—should he try to cut off the shot before it reaches the back of the court, or should he wait, in the hope that the ball will rebound far enough for him to take a swing at it? Either way, this is defensive thinking—and you have forced it upon him. Either way, you have got him away from the middle of the court, which means that you are playing a successful tactical game.

In going for a length down the nearest side wall aim for a spot about 3 ft. above the tin and hit the ball hard enough to make it bounce in or close to the nick within two or three yards of the back wall. The point of the high clearance above the tin is that if you hit too low, the ball will bounce so far forward that your opponent will be able to intercept. To hit *gently* to a good length, obviously you must aim higher

59

up the front wall. When you learn how to "cut" the ball, this will help you to achieve a good length. As for the good length cross-court shots, these tend to be easier to intercept or retrieve, since they have farther to travel and, for much of the way, are well clear of the side walls. So use cross-court shots sparingly.

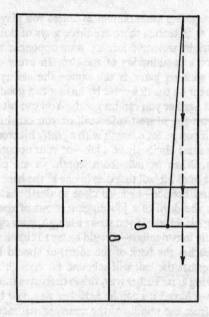

Figure 4 A length shot played on the forehand.

DO: Face the side wall. Play off the correct foot. Get your shoulder down. Lift the head of the racket above the level of the wrist. Bend the knee of the front leg. During the stroke, keep the body relaxed but still, the racket face open. Keep your eye on the ball at all times.

Finally, as a good length is the basis of your game, make it your first priority as you adjust to the court and the ball during the knock-up and early in the match itself. If your opponent is anywhere near your own standard, then the first man to strike a length will gain the initiative.

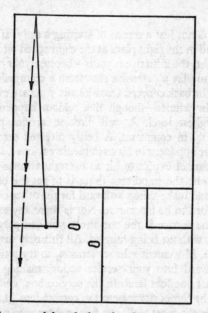

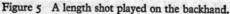

Figure 5 A length shot played on the backhand.

DON'T: Face the front wall. Play off the wrong foot. Stand too close to the ball. Let your shoulder come up. Stand upright. Move your feet before the stroke is completed. Drop the head of the racket. Lift your head.

Note: The advice ("Do" and "Don't") applies to both forehand and backhand.

Service

A service is not just a means of starting a rally. If you can put the ball in the right place at the right speed on the right line of flight, the initiative is yours—because your opponent will have to play a defensive shot from a cramped position in one of the back corners. Occasionally you may even serve an outright winner—though this seldom happens at the game's highest level. A well directed service puts you momentarily in command. A badly directed service may enable your opponent to hit an immediate winner. It follows that you cannot expect to hit an outright winner with the service itself: the important thing is to get the ball safely into play and make things awkward for the other chap. You cannot afford to be inaccurate. Nor is there any excuse for it, since the service is the one stroke you can play in your own time, without being hurried. All this may make you a little tense. Movement releases tension, so try walking two paces forward into your service action, making sure (a) that at least one foot lands in the service box, and (b) that your weight comes down onto the correct foot (that is, the foot nearer the front wall). At first, concentrate on serving forehand from both service boxes. When you can do this competently, develop a backhand service. This done, there is quite a lot of variety at your disposal. But first, the forehand service . . .

The rules demand that, when serving, you must have at least one foot on the floor within the service box and not touching the lines marking its boundaries. The ball must be hit directly onto the front wall above the cut line. Its first bounce (unless your opponent volleys it) must be in the opposite court, though the ball may hit the side wall or the back wall (or both) before it bounces.

Right. Let's get organized. Your stance at the moment of impact is the first thing to settle, because you will swing along a line parallel with an imaginary line from the toes of one foot to the toes of the other. You are serving forehand, remember. We will start in the right-hand box. As an experiment, adopt the same stance as that for the forehand drive, facing the side wall and hitting the ball when it is somewhere on the shortest line between your left foot and the right-hand side wall. But this time your body is upright and you hit the ball while it is at, or just below, eye level. Aim left for a spot about 3 ft. above the cut line. The ball will then rebound down the middle of the court. If it lands in your own service court, it is a fault. If it lands in your opponent's, he will murder it. So you have to adjust your angle, aiming nearer the middle of the front wall. To do this, turn your feet and body slightly to the left, towards the front wall. You still toss up the ball over your left foot. This time the ball will rebound nearer the left-hand side wall. But it may still offer your opponent an easy volley—or a full-blooded backhand drive if your service is so weak that it drops just over the short line. So turn a little more. Experiment until direction, height, and length are perfect—which means that, after clearing the short line, the ball strikes the left-hand side wall and dies in the back corner. Your opponent will have no chance to volley unless he stretches to hit the ball before it goes onto the side wall. Nor will he have room to play a respectable drive. So the initiative is yours.

The pace and arc of the service depend on your service action. The direction of the service depends on your stance. You will probably find the best stance brings you facing the vicinity of the front right-hand corner. But experiment until you get it right. And aim for a particular spot on the front wall: this will most likely be about 3 ft. above the cut

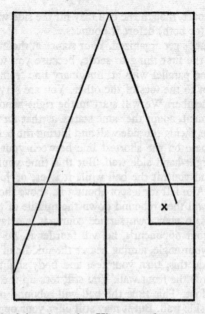

Figure 6   A length service. Hit at a moderate pace with the
face of the racket open.

Note: Immediately after serving, always go to midcourt,
with your body square to the front wall but your head turned
to watch the ball and your opponent. This also applies to the
other types of service—see figures 7–10.

line, depending on how hard you hit. Always aim low at the
beginning of the first game, until you get your eye in. Then
gradually go higher.

Now move over to the left-hand service box and, still
serving forehand, go through the same routine. The difference now is that, in turning your stance to achieve the best
angle, you turn to the right—away from the front wall,
instead of towards it. Again, practice until you can serve

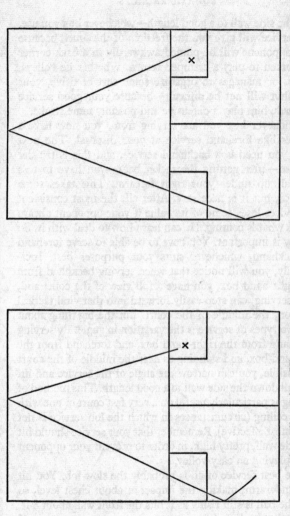

Figure 7 A side wall service. Hit at a moderate pace to strike the side wall high up and well forward. This prevents hand-out from volleying before the ball has struck the side wall.

Figure 8 A lob service. Similar in direction to a length service. But this is a gentle stroke making the ball rise high onto the front wall, then striking high on the side wall, and dropping into the back corner.

onto the side wall to a good length—whichever box you use, this service will give you the freedom of the court, because your opponent will be pinned awkwardly in a back corner and forced to play a cramped return. Whether he volleys, boasts, or manages to organize some sort of drive, your next shot will not be difficult—because your good service has made him play a defensive and possibly tame stroke.

Whichever box you are serving from, you now have a businesslike forehand service at your disposal. The next thing you need is a backhand service, and this is trickier because—*after* getting the racket back—you have to toss the ball up under your right forearm. This takes some practice, but it is necessary. After all, the most consistent of services loses some of its value if your opponent always knows what is coming. He can learn how to deal with it. So variety is important. You have to be able to serve forehand or backhand, whichever suits your purposes best. Incidentally, you will notice that when serving backhand from the right-hand box, you have a full view of the court and, after serving, can step easily forward into that vital tactical position, the middle of the court. But the big thing about the two types of service is the variation in angle. By serving backhand from the right-hand box, and forehand from the left-hand box, and standing as near the middle of the court as possible, you can narrow the angle of the service and hit the ball down the side wall to a good length. This method of serving is particularly useful on a very fast court or one with a low ceiling (circumstances in which the lob service is not at its most effective). Remember that your service should hit the side wall, pretty high, in order to prevent your opponent from playing an easy volley.

The best service of all is probably the slow lob. You hit this underarm, making the impact at about chest level, so that the ball is still rising as it hits the front wall about 8 ft. above the cut line. Then it soars over your opponent and drops sharply to die in the back corner. If possible, it should

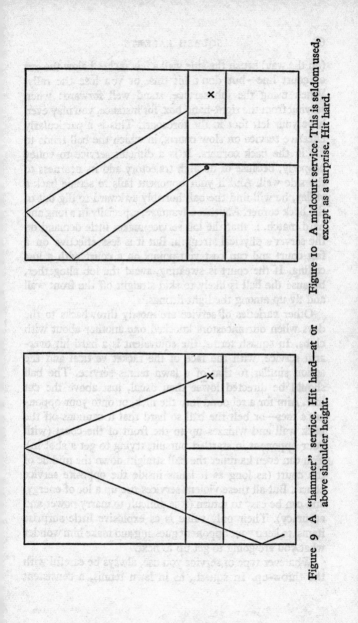

Figure 10   A midcourt service. This is seldom used, except as a surprise. Hit hard.

Figure 9   A "hammer" service. Hit hard—at or above shoulder height.

(on the way) brush the side wall a few inches below the out of court line—but don't hit this, or you lose the rally. When using the lob service, stand well forward: when serving from the right-hand box, for instance, you may even have your left foot in the forecourt. This is a particularly effective service on slow courts, in which the ball tends to die in the back corners. It is a difficult service to volley properly, because of its high trajectory and its nearness to the side wall. And if your opponent fails to scrape back a volley, he will find the ball horribly awkward to dig out of the back corner. Another advantage, especially in a long and hard match, is that the lob service makes little demand on the server's physical strength. But it is less effective on a fast court and can cost you points on a court with a low ceiling. If the court is sweating, avoid the lob altogether, because the ball is likely to skid straight off the front wall and fly up among the light fittings.

Other varieties of service are mostly throwbacks to the days when our ancestors knocked one another about with clubs. In squash terms, the equivalent is a hard hit over-arm service, with the face of the racket vertical and the action similar to that of a lawn tennis service. The ball should be directed lower than usual, just above the cut line. Aim for a rebound into the nick, or onto your opponent's toes—or belt the ball so hard that it cannons off the back wall and whizzes up to the front of the court (with your opponent in startled pursuit, trying to get a shot in). You can even hammer the ball straight down the middle of the court (as long as it lands inside the opposite service court). But all these violent services use up a lot of energy, and can be easy to return (it is difficult to marry power and accuracy). Their only value is as explosive little surprise items, to keep your opponent guessing and make him wonder what you are going to get up to next.

Whatever type of service you use, always be careful with the throw-up. In squash, as in lawn tennis, a consistent throw-up is a vital component of a consistent service. Throw the ball up slightly beyond the toes of whichever foot is nearest the front wall. Exactly how high you make the impact is largely up to you, though we have indicated the three main positions—about eye level for straightforward services, nearer the chest for lob services, and about a foot above eye level if you want to use the heavy artillery.

At this point we do not want to delve too deeply into tactical issues. But never forget the usefulness of varying your services. Start by serving low, to get your eyes and touch adjusted. Then try a few variations—and remember that your opponent will spot big variations more easily than he will spot the little ones. Every time you start serving you can choose whichever service box you prefer. After that you serve from each box alternately until you lose a rally. Make your opponent play as many returns as possible from the flank he likes least. Vary pace, angle, height, and length, partly to keep the poor chap in a continual state of anxiety, partly to find out what sort of stuff he least likes dealing with—and give him plenty of that, especially when you are most in need of points.

Angle

The walls give squash some attractive special qualities. One is obvious: they stop the ball getting out. At the end of a rally no one has to go ball-hunting, because it is never far away. But besides keeping the roof up and the ball within reach, the side walls have other, more rewarding uses. They give squash an inimitable and engrossing character and play important roles in the battle of wits the game provides—because rebounds make possible all sorts of subtle, high-speed geometry in both attack and defence. At first the angles at which the ball flies about will be confusing, because you cannot relate them to any other game you have played. You have moved into a new and exciting world. Experience will soon teach you what to expect: and there is no substitute for experience. You have to live with the angles to get to know them. But getting accustomed to the angles, and learning to make tactical use of the side walls, is wonderfully satisfying. It takes the game into a different dimension.

There are three recognized side-wall shots—the angle, the reverse angle, and the boast. The first two are attacking shots, the third defensive. We will deal with the angle first. Though its purpose is offensive, its nature is delicate rather than violent. The ball travels from your racket onto the nearest side wall, rebounding to and from the front wall, to die near the farthest side wall (in the nick, if you're lucky). It *has* to die near the farthest side wall, because if it rebounds from that wall into the middle of the court, your opponent will arrive in time to play his return without undue anxiety. This would defeat the object of the shot and leave you at your opponent's mercy. So play the angle in such a way that the ball's first bounce is close to the nick below the farthest side wall. Ideally, the ball will travel low all the way. But the height you give it—and the strength with which you hit it—obviously depend on your position in the court. The farther back you are, the more pace and lift the shot needs (and the more difficult it is to play the angle accurately and effectively). In assessing the amount of pace needed, remember that in striking the side wall the ball will lose some of its speed. However far forward you are, or however far back, you should not be more than two yards from the side wall when you play the angle. Otherwise your opponent will have time to "read" and anticipate the shot and you will have to get out of his way, putting yourself out of position in the process. Experiment with your stance, and with the strength and lift of the stroke. Get your touch adjusted so that the ball dies where you want it to.

Your stance is like that for the ordinary drive, though the body and feet are turned slightly more away from the front wall. Save for this small variation, the stroke is the ordinary forehand or backhand drive, with the wrist open (bent backwards and upwards) and the head of the racket up. Swing on a line parallel with the imaginary line from the toes of one foot to the toes of the other. On impact, the ball will again be on a straight line between the front foot (that nearest the front wall) and the part of the side wall to which the toes of that foot are pointing. Get right across to the ball. Don't lunge. Bend your knee and get down to the stroke. Immediately after impact, "push off" on your way back to the middle of the court.

The angle can have either of two basic purposes. One is to manœuvre your opponent out of position. The other is to make a winner when he is already out of position—behind you (on the same side of the court) or backing hastily in that direction after he has played a shot from the front of the court. For example, when you have forced your opponent to boast, an angle is one way of exploiting the advantage

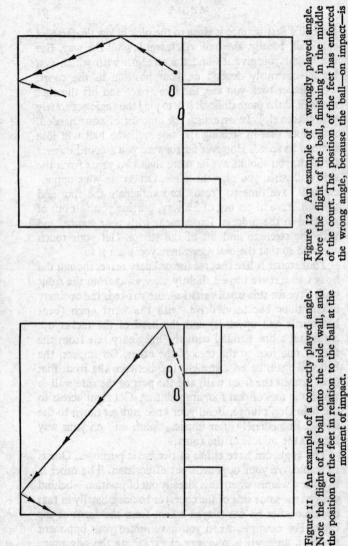

Figure 11 An example of a correctly played angle. Note the flight of the ball onto the side wall, and the position of the feet in relation to the ball at the moment of impact.

Figure 12 An example of a wrongly played angle. Note the flight of the ball, finishing in the middle of the court. The position of the feet has enforced the wrong angle, because the ball—on impact—is

thus gained. It then comes into its own as a surprise item. The position and stance from which you play it may lead your opponent to expect a drive to a length (either down the side wall or across court), a lob, or a straight drop shot for the nearest front corner. The angle offers you yet another choice—another way to catch your man unprepared, and moving the wrong way. Its effect is much the same as that of the drop shot: to bring your opponent racing up to the front of the court (probably too late, if you have played the shot the right way at the right time). Its advantage over the drop shot is that it is more likely to catch your opponent on the wrong foot: as he heads for one front corner, anticipating a drop shot, your angle towards the other front corner may even catch him cross-legged ... besides costing him the rally, this will do his morale no good at all.

Reverse Angle

This is hit across court to the farthest side wall, rebounding to and from the front wall, to die near the side wall from which you are playing the shot. Like the angle, it is a surprise item which can lure your opponent out of position, or catch him on the wrong foot and make you a winner—if the shot is played accurately. The reverse angle is sometimes used in returning a poor service. It is then an effective way of getting your opponent away from the middle of the court: moreover, it will put him on edge, because he will have to let the ball come across the court, in front of him, before he sets off to pursue it to the far side of the court. In other words, he will start late. This illustrates the difference between expectation (what we think is likely to happen) and anticipation (the action we take in preparation). If your opponent hits a poor service he may expect a reverse angle but he cannot anticipate it, because if he moves before the ball goes across him, he will move straight into its path and risk getting perforated. The reverse angle should not be attempted when your opponent is in the front of the court, unless he is hurrying backwards (simple tactics—if your opponent is moving, put the ball in the area he is running away from).

Compared with the stance for the drive, your body and feet are now turned slightly more towards the front wall. With good wrist work you may be able to shorten your backswing yet still hit hard, giving no indication of your intentions, and thus increasing the element of surprise. The position of the ball at impact is important and—compared with almost every other stroke in the game—unusual.

Because the ball is between your body and the front wall, not the side wall. At the moment of impact the line between your front foot (the one nearest the front wall), the ball, and the front wall is parallel with the side wall. When you

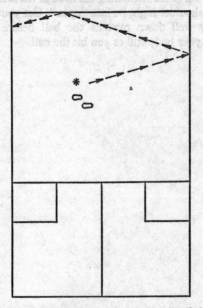

Figure 13 An example of a correctly played backhand reverse angle. Note that, on impact, the ball is between the leading foot (in the case of a backhand, the right foot) and the front wall.

practise the shot it will be obvious why you have to take the ball in this position. It will also be obvious that you are playing *across* the line of flight; that hitting the opposite side wall takes so much speed off the ball that it may go down before reaching the front wall; that in these circumstances it would be optimistic to expect consistent accuracy; and that the reverse angle is therefore a stroke to use sparingly. It is, as it were, one of the luxuries of the game rather than a "bread and butter" shot. For all that, make the stroke part of your repertory. Take care in playing it. At the top of the backswing the head of the racket should be about shoulder high, its face "open". Get your shoulder and body well down towards the ball before impact—and keep your body still as you hit the ball.

Boast

A competent opponent will explore the back corners persistently, especially when he is serving. So you will often have to hit the ball while it is hovering about between you and a back corner—while the front wall is out of sight. In this situation you cannot play the ball direct onto the front wall. You should not even try to do so. Have the discretion to admit that a boast, a defensive shot, has been forced upon you. It is the only way to dig otherwise irretrievable shots out of the back corners. Often you will have to look sharp to achieve even a boast, though when receiving service you will be handily placed to get into position for the stroke. The shot comes in three varieties—single boast, double boast, and back-wall boast. By far the most frequent (so much so that the word "boast" on its own is commonly used to describe it) is the

Single boast

This is almost an angle shot in its direction, though it is played from farther back in the court. The ball is hit hard, upwards, onto the nearest side wall, rebounding across the court onto the front wall, then falling to die in or close to the nick below the opposite side wall—so that ultimately the shot has an effect similar to that of an angle or cross-court drop. Playing a boast demands strict attention to stance: facing the *back* wall, with your body at a right-angle to the side wall and (on the forehand) your left foot about 2 ft. from the side wall. Though it depends on how quickly you have been able to get into position, that left foot will be almost parallel with the side wall and pointing towards

77

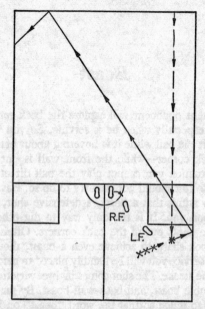

Figure 14   An example of a correctly played boast (forehand).
This shows probably the most forward position from which
you will be forced to boast. You are properly positioned in
mid-court (within the half-circle illustrated) when your
opponent plays a shot that passes you and seems destined to
die at the back of the court. So it has to be intercepted. Take a
step with your right foot, pivoting at the same time, to bring
your weight down on your left foot. You are now facing the
back corner (on the forehand side). Note the position of
your left foot in relation to the ball.

the back corner. This is the only stance from which you
have room to exploit a normal swing and the power it
provides. So it is essential to turn your back on the front
wall and get your body round and down—you must obviously get your racket under the ball if you are to hit
upwards. There is nothing tricky about the swing itself—it

is the stroke used for the ordinary drive. On impact the ball will be between the *side* wall and your left foot (on the forehand) and between the side wall and your right foot on the backhand. Make sure that you get your foot beside the

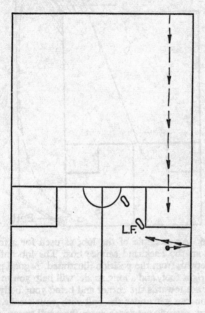

Figure 15 An example of an unsuccessful attempt to boast. Note the position of the left foot. If you fail to swing that foot round far enough, the ball will be well past you, leaving you no hope of getting the ball to the front wall.

ball: to do this you will usually have to get to the back of the court in a hurry. So if you anticipate the need for a boast, move fast.

As you will be in a corner, it is essential that, immediately after impact, you push back (off your left foot on the forehand, off your right foot on the backhand) towards the

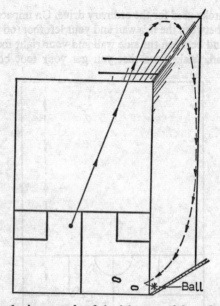

Figure 16 An example of the lob, as used for a forehand service from the backhand service box. The lob enforces a boasted return, from the position illustrated. A good push off from the right foot, and a long stride, will help you to stretch your left foot towards the corner and bring your body down, so that you can get under the ball with your stroke. In the case shown, there is not much room for a full swing, so your stroke will be shorter than usual and the wrist will have to play its part. You play the ball up onto the side wall, so that the ball then sails up, across the court, and drops into the front corner (on the backhand side of the court). Be satisfied to get the ball up and keep it in play: remember that you are on the defensive.

middle of the court. A swift recovery may be difficult (because you have been forced out of position, into a corner), but it is necessary. After all, a boast travels on a long journey and takes some time to reach its destination. Your opponent is hardly likely to be caught napping. He can anticipate where your boast is heading and, even if it arrives bang on target, he should get there in ample time to play his next shot. So unless, having boasted, you nip back to the middle of the court like lightning, he will have you at his mercy.

We may as well face the fact that at almost every level of the game the ultimate destination of a boast often depends as much on luck as it does on technique. The boast is, in fact, a calculated risk. But frequently it is the only stroke you can attempt, because nothing else is "on". It may go down, or offer your opponent an easy kill. But it should enable you to keep the rally going and draw your opponent to the front of the court (out of position) while you hustle up to the middle of the court, ready to seize the slightest chance of regaining the initiative. With luck a good boast may even turn out to be a winning "nick". One way and another, it can be a firm friend in time of trouble, and happily it is easy to practise: go to a back corner, organize your stance, drop the ball, and bang away. Keep at it until you achieve control over the shot.

Double boast

This time the ball hits the nearest side wall and rebounds first onto the other side wall, then onto the front wall, before falling to its death. Geometric precision of this nature is deliberately attempted only by absent-minded megalomaniacs ... the sort who, in football, try to score goals from the halfway line. So the double boast is seldom, if ever, played on purpose. It happens by accident.

Back-wall boast

You cannot get more defensive than this. There is even a school of thought who consider that the shot should be banned altogether, since (they say) it is an admission of defeat. This is nonsense. The shot is perfectly legal and on rare occasions may keep a rally going when there is nothing else to try—when not even a single boast is possible. The back-wall boast means that you have been convicted and sentenced, but are appealing for a reprieve in the hope of a pardon. It remains the black sheep of the boast family. It is not really a boast at all: rather a lob in reverse. The back-wall boast occurs only when the ball has beaten you to the back of the court. But as you hare after the ball you notice that for a second—either just before the ball reaches the back wall, or just after rebounding from it—you can get in a shot. So you hit the ball upwards onto the back wall in the hope that it will carry to the front wall before bouncing. This is the only shot in squash which is played when the ball is between the striker and the back wall. As we say, it is a lob in reverse, so there should be no need for violence. One last point. Never regard the back-wall boast as a substitute for correct positioning. If there is the slightest chance of getting into position in time to play a constructive shot, do so. Don't hang about, ponderously idle, using the back-wall boast to save your legs and lungs. It is sloppy squash and will never do you much good.

Drop Shot

A golfer can play a good round with only four clubs, because he knows which clubs are essential and which are not. In the same way squash can be reduced to four basic shots —drive, drop shot, angle, and lob (probably in that order of importance). You can play these strokes in various ways, and you can add others to your armoury: but you will get nowhere as a squash player until you have mastered "the big four". The drive and the angle we have already discussed. Now we can turn to the silent weapon that kills by stealth—the drop shot. This is played gently but firmly onto the front wall, just above the tin, towards either corner. It should be slightly angled so that, after rebounding from the front wall, it falls immediately to die in the nick. Even if the ball misses the nick, it should cling closely to the side wall and therefore be difficult to return. It is such a soft little shot that the ball should bounce twice before your opponent can reach it. Always play the drop shot to a corner, where it is more difficult to deal with and more effective in getting your opponent out of position.

A slow ball and a cold court provide the ideal conditions for a perfect drop shot. It will seldom be a winner on a hot court unless it is played with flawless control—or unless a tiring opponent has first been drawn well out of position. But this question of first getting the opponent out of position, at the back of the court, is vital to successful use of the drop shot in any conditions. (A drive to a length, followed by a drop shot to the diagonally opposite front corner, is a piece of basic tactics for forcing your opponent to cover the maximum distance in the minimum time.)

If you have made your opponent boast, a drop shot is the obvious way to press home your advantage. Just as obvious is the value of a drop shot when your opponent is tiring and can no longer get up the court quickly: a few drop shots will then use up the last dregs of his energy, and break his heart too. Never play a drop shot when your opponent is in front of you, unless he is hurrying backwards at such a rate that the sudden need to stop and go forwards may be beyond him. The drop shot, in short, has two fundamental uses, both of them offensive: to get your opponent out of position, or to finish him off when he is already out of position.

The shot can be effectively disguised by adjustments in your wrist action. This will make it difficult for your opponent to anticipate which corner your drop shot is going to. He may even expect a lob, since your positioning, and the way you lean forward towards the ball, are much the same for both shots. In fact, as far as your opponent is concerned, no fewer than seven shots are "on"—a straight drop shot, a drop shot angled off the side wall, a cross-court drop, a lob, an angle, a straight drive, or a cross-court drive. So that when you move into position to play a drop shot, the other chap can never be sure what you are up to. Just one word of warning: before learning to mask your intentions by subtle wrist-work, concentrate on mastering the basic weapon, the drop shot towards the nearest front corner. Because this is the one we are talking about when we say the drop is among the game's four essential strokes.

The front of the court is the best place for launching drop shots. We can be even more specific and outline an imaginary box from which these shots should be played. The back of the box is the short line. The front is parallel with the short line, but three yards nearer the front wall. The sides of our box are imaginary continuations—towards the front wall—of the inner lines of the service boxes. This

5   Heather McKay (Australia) moves in to play a backhand. Good points:
eyes on ball; correct grip; shoulders in line with feet; body—turned back to
give maximum pivot and punch on impact—coming over right foot.
Criticism: the straight leg (instead of a bent knee) means that she has to come
down on her heel instead of her toes, and therefore has no means of pushing
    back after playing the stroke; racket much too high for start of stroke.

6 Heather McKay (Australia) plays a low backhand. Good points: eyes on ball; footwork perfect, with weight on front foot, and knee bent; racket face open; back of hand on top of handle.

7   Ibrahim Amin (Egypt) plays a backhand to a shot—from David Brazier
(Britain)—that has passed him. Criticism: Amin should be boasting off the
side wall instead of trying to play the ball direct to the front wall; in the
attempt to get the ball round he has turned over his wrist and the head of the
racket; Brazier's thumb should be round the handle—instead it is lying along
the top, pressing the head of the racket down. Good point: he is looking at
what is going on behind him.

8   Dick Carter (Australia)—playing Aftab Jawaid (Pakistan)—has moved from midcourt to play a ball that has passed him and is heading towards the back corner. Good points: Carter, thrusting his shoulder towards the corner, has stretched his leg well, distributed his weight properly, and got well down, so that his racket will start low and come up under the ball; his wrist is on top so that the head of the racket must be open; Jawaid is still watching the ball.

sounds complicated, but it is not: once on court, you can easily work out where the "drop shot box" is situated. And whenever the course of a rally brings you into that area, you will know that a drop shot is "on", as long as the other chap is out of position. Newcomers to the game should never attempt a drop shot from farther back than the service boxes, and seldom from even that far back. It is a difficult shot to play accurately from the back of the court,

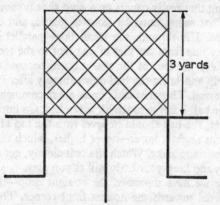

3 yards

Figure 17 The imaginary "box" illustrating the area from which drop shots are usually played.

and the novice who ignores this warning will find "long" drops a costly investment. But if you are in good form, and the game is firmly in your control, try a long drop as an experiment. If it comes off, your opponent will react like a startled rabbit. But basically these long drops require a natural aptitude plus a perfect touch. They are best left alone until your game has thoroughly matured.

The drop shot should never be played in a hurry, because immaculate control is essential. So get into position quickly, and steady yourself before stroking the ball. Do not run directly towards the ball—run so that, as usual, you get the ball between you and the side wall before impact. (If you do make the mistake of running directly towards the ball, it will be between you and the front wall when you play it—this means you will be forced to play a cross-court shot, or risk dislodging a kneecap in the attempt to play straight.) Having arrived in the right place, adopt the stance you would adopt for a drive. You may use a full swing, to keep your opponent guessing until the last second. But the part of a swing that really counts on a drop shot is shorter than usual. That swing must be smooth, gentle, and carefully controlled. Hit through the usual line—parallel with an imaginary line from the toes of one foot to the toes of the other. Keep the face of the racket open, because this will apply spin and bring the ball down sharply after it has hit the front wall. The wrist and fingers are in command all the way. The ball is not so much hit as stroked. On impact with the racket, the ball should be level with the top of the tin, or perhaps slightly lower—never higher, which makes the drop shot more risky. Watch the ball closely, get down to the shot, and keep your body still as you play.

So far we have discussed the straight drop—that is, a drop played towards the nearest front corner. This is the basic drop, a vital component of your game. Practice is easy: start near the front wall, get your touch right, and once you can play the shot accurately gradually move back until you are practising it from the vicinity of the short line. When you can use this shot effectively in match play, you can begin to develop one or two variations. The obvious one is the cross-court drop, played towards the most distant front corner, with the ball brushing the front wall on the way. In this case (as in playing a reverse angle) your stance brings you round to face the side wall, but at the moment of impact the ball is between you and the front wall. The angle of your approach to the ball normally dictates whether your drop shot is played straight or cross-court (and the angle of your approach may sometimes be dictated by your opponent). Once you have the hang of both the straight and cross-court drops, you will learn to disguise your intentions by subtle little variations in stance and wrist-work. But master the simple things— basic squash—before you start messing about with the clever stuff, which in any case will be seldom used. Another crafty but terribly difficult variant is a top-spin drop shot played as a half-volley. This requires such faultless timing that it happens more often by accident than design. Often you will play a drop shot on the volley. This is very risky if the ball is travelling fast, because the consummate control you need is almost impossible. Even when the ball is travelling at a moderate speed, the volleyed drop shot demands perfect positioning and stroke control.

One last important note. The straight drop shot often causes lets or collisions. This is because a man who has played a drop shot naturally wants to get back to the middle of the court by the shortest possible route, as he does after playing any shot. But in the case of a drop shot, that shortest possible route will find him backing away towards mid-court while the opponent is travelling on the same path in the opposite direction—in order to return the drop shot, which is hovering about in the front corner. The man who played the drop shot is at fault. After playing the shot his first move should not be backwards, but side-ways, towards the side wall that is farthest away from the ball. Then, having thus left his opponent a clear path to the ball, he can back towards mid-court. (Never turn your back on the front wall after playing a drop shot.) The recovery route, in fact, is not a straight line, but a curve, first parallel with the front wall, then at a right angle to it. The player who is good at drop shots will lose many of the advantages they bring him unless he observes the right-of-way by using this curved recovery. If he fails to observe that right-of-way, his opponent will be awarded a let or a penalty point.

Volley

The volley comes in many varieties, because during a rally the word covers all shots played before the ball touches the floor. So you can play an angled volley, a drop volley, and so on. The stroke is a volley because you hit the ball at a particular *time*; it becomes an angled or drop volley because you hit it in a particular *way*. Most of your volleys (except when returning service) will be played from the vicinity of the short line. This usually means taking the ball early, when its pace is normally faster—and the arc of its flight less predictable—than is the case after a bounce. Small wonder that volleys provide every match with the bulk of its mistakes. There are so many possibilities of error when volleying that you should not be too ambitious in your intentions. As a preliminary safety precaution, aim about 6 in. above the tin—no lower—if you are attempting a winner. The vital thing is to keep your eye on the ball, to watch the ball right onto the racket. In addition, quick footwork is essential, whether you are moving forwards, backwards, or sideways. In short, make up your mind; get into position fast; steady yourself; and watch the ball, like a hawk. Don't make the mistake (common to many ball games) of looking at the place to which you intend to hit the ball. This spells error. Instead, look at the ball itself.

Now for the volley's uses. These can be roughly grouped under three main headings—attacking, defensive, and tactical. In attack, the volley enables you to intercept a cross-court drive, thus suddenly increasing the pace of a rally and taking your opponent by surprise (perhaps on the wrong foot). The volley also helps you to maintain a fast pace against an opponent who prefers a slower game. If he is out of position, a well-placed volley may even give you an outright winner. In defence, when you are caught out of position in the front of the court, or on the wrong foot, a volley can cut off a shot that is passing you and looks like finding a good length in one of the back corners—a shot that, once past you, would be difficult or even impossible to return. The same thing applies when, farther back in the court, you have to return a service that looks like dropping on a perfect length. Another defensive use of the volley is, of course, on those odd occasions when you are scrambling about in the front of the court and suddenly find the ball coming straight at you off the front wall. Tactically, the volley's main uses are to help you to speed up the game, stay in mid-court, and cut down the amount of running you have to do. But to play this sort of game consistently, you need to be a bit of an acrobat, with fast reflexes and a sure touch (just as in tennis the good doubles players, who excel in those quickfire exchanges at the net, are the people with the fastest reflexes). The volley also has a less exciting but more essential tactical role: in returning service (especially the lob service) it is often the only stroke you can play; but, if well placed, it will help you to take over the mid-court position that is the hub of tactical supremacy.

When you play a volley deliberately (as distinct from the volley that is forced upon you), try to set yourself as you would for an ordinary drive—facing the side wall. Get into position quickly, then stand still, knees bent . . . your stillness is that of a tiger poised for the spring. Remember that as you get into position your racket must do the same— —drawn back, in readiness for the stroke. Otherwise you will "snatch" at the ball and bungle the shot. At the start of the stroke your upper arm should be near the body. Your swing depends on the speed with which the ball is coming your way, and where you want to put it. But on the whole your swing will be shorter than usual. To get the control you need, it is important to keep the wrist low, with the head of the racket well above the wrist. Lean forward into the shot. Smack the ball when it is between you and the side wall. As you play the stroke, your weight moves from the back foot to the front foot.

When there is no need to apply pace and you want to play a gentle volley onto the front wall—the drop volley— all you really require is a firm push at the ball. Cut the ball downwards so that it will die quickly after rebounding from the front wall. Experience will teach you to play the drop volley only off a slow-moving ball, and to apply both cut and slice to hasten the ball's death.

This bring us to the stop volley, which you need on those occasions when the ball is coming at you like a bullet —carrying the twin dangers that you will be utterly beaten if the ball passes you, or perforated if it doesn't. It should go without saying that there is hardly any swing to this shot: for one thing, you have no time. All you can do is to try for a drop shot, keeping your wrist firm and letting the ball hit a "dead" racket. Obviously this is a difficult shot to play well. It demands fast reflexes and a sure touch.

Another form of the volley is the smash, similar to that in tennis. There is always a tendency to be violent when playing a high volley, but they are usually awkward shots to play, and in any case placing is more important than power. The ball, we repeat, must be watched right onto the racket. If you are lucky enough to find the ball coming your way at just the right height and speed for a full-blooded smash, remember this: you will not put the ball "away" unless your placing is sensible and accurate. The side-wall smash, in which you use the nearest side wall to deflect the course of your shot, can be an effective surprise item. But it is difficult to play accurately—and in squash, accuracy is more important than naked violence. It follows that to play a smash with any degree of safety, you need to be in the front of the court. To attempt a winning smash from the back of the court makes about as much sense as driving round a hairpin bend at 50 miles an hour.

Half-volley

The basic, orthodox strokes are all played either before or after the ball has bounced. The half-volley is the tricky customer in the middle. It is a hybrid shot, springing from momentary inspiration or need. After all, you can hardly base your whole strategy on playing shots as the ball is just coming off the floor: if squash was slow enough and simple enough to permit that sort of thinking, it would hardly be worth playing. So the half-volley is never planned more than a second in advance. It just happens . . . when you and the ball get together in a handy proximity. By a "handy proximity" we mean the sort of situation that occurs in cricket when a batsman gets body and bat right to the pitch of the ball so that he can drive it, almost off his toes (the most horrifying example is, of course, the attempted "yorker"). To carry the cricket parallel a little further, it is important to keep your head down. Otherwise all you will feel of the ball is the draught it makes going by.

The half-volley is useful in both attack and defence. In attack it can be used to take the ball early and thus speed up the game, surprising your opponent and perhaps catching him out of position. In defence, the half-volley is sometimes forced upon you when—out of position, with no time for a more orthodox stroke—you need to intercept a shot that would otherwise leave you stranded. It will then keep the rally going and give you time to recover to mid-court. In these circumstances it is obviously played in a hurry and demands perfect timing if it is to be constructive.

But let us assume that you are using the half-volley deliberately, as a means of attack. First (again, like the cricketer), you must move your feet to the ball. The half-volley is played closer to the floor, and closer to your feet, than any other shot. It follows that you have to get your head down (not your body) so that you can watch the ball onto the racket: in squash, as in cricket and golf, the consequences are disastrous if your head is up instead of down when you try to make contact with the ball. As for the drive, face the side wall. The head of the racket is open. Your racket swings so low that it will probably touch the floor, so the hand governing the racket will also be low (in this one isolated case we will not insist on having the wrist *below* the head of the racket, since this would involve the time-consuming bore of taking up the floorboards). But let us not be too frivolous. The wrist is supple, and in complete control of the shot. The weight, as usual, moves from the back foot to the front foot. Impact occurs as the ball leaves the floor—and at that split-second the ball should be bang in line between your front foot and the side wall. If you fail to hit the ball at the bottom of the swing and level with your foot, the ball will fly up and probably offer your opponent an easy volley. Follow straight through, just as you would in cricket.

When you spot the chance for a powerful, attacking half-volley, put every other shot out of your mind, decide exactly where you want to send the ball, and then whip it away. Let yourself go. Not that the half-volley's attacking uses are necessarily violent. The shorter the swing, the more delicate the stroke. As your experience grows and your touch improves, you can develop half-volley drop shots and even half-volley angles (the angles need a sharper tap than the drops, and are less likely to be bungled). But these two are "luxury" shots and are not recommended for beginners. Even advanced players are well advised to have a few points in hand before risking such clever little embellishments.

Lob

Like the drive, drop shot, and angle, the lob is one of the
four strokes essential to your game. In its arc, direction, and
speed it is rather like a lob service. Its purpose is to soar
slowly over your opponent (and his racket), travelling just
fast enough to reach one of the back corners, where it falls
sharply and dies. The lob is a firm prop to lean on when you
are in trouble, and it has many tactical uses. First, if you
have been drawn hurriedly to the front of the court, you
need time to recover to mid-court, because you cannot
afford to leave your opponent with an open court while you
are scrambling about in one of the front corners. The lob
will give you the time you need, because it keeps the ball
in the air for a long while. Second, if you are playing a
hustler who is better than you are when it comes to playing
a fast game, the lob will deny him the speed he thrives on.
Instead, repeated use of the lob will force him to play
defensively. Third, occasional use of the lob enables you
to vary the pace and flight of the ball during a rally, thus
upsetting your opponent's rhythm. Fourth, there are times
when mind and body both need a breather—when your
legs are tiring and a rally needs "rethinking" because it is
getting out of your control. The lob gives you the respite
you need. Fifth, the lob is one way of forcing your opponent
into a back corner while you take over the important midcourt position. Sixth, the lob can make your opponent run
while you save energy.

From all this, you will gather that the lob earns its keep
in many ways, though its basic value is defensive. Height
and a good length are obviously essential if the lob is to

elude your opponent's racket and die in a back corner. If
you play the lob well, your opponent can attempt only one
shot, a volley. If he cannot manage this, his only hope is that
he will have enough room to hit the ball after it has bounced
in the back corner. Even if the lob does not quite clear your
opponent's racket, the chances are that his volley will be
played rather wildly, at full stretch—and while the ball is
reaching him you will have a second or two in which to
start off towards mid-court. But a rank bad lob that comes
within easy reach of your opponent will, of course, be
banged away so fast that you may be able to do nothing
about it. So accuracy is vital—especially in giving the ball
height early in its flight.

The best and safest lob is played cross-court, to brush the
side wall (about 1 ft. below the out of court line and 4 ft.
from the back wall) before dying. You can also lob straight
down (and close to) the nearest side wall—but be wary of the
obvious danger that, at the top of its flight, the ball may
go out of court. The cross-court lob is safer because it
avoids this danger: at the highest point of its arc, the cross-
court lob will be over the middle of the court, far away from
any of the out of court lines. All you have to watch out for
are the lights and any girders.

The lob can be played from anywhere, but is most effective from the front of the court. When played from the back
it is rather obvious—though even then it can serve a useful
purpose, not least in shifting your opponent from the midcourt position you want to take over from him. As we said
in the chapter on the drop shot, your positioning and stance
for a lob would permit six other shots. For example, your
opponent may anticipate a drop shot and start moving
forward: an unexpected lob forces him to change quickly
into reverse gear. Because the shoulder of the racket arm
falls more naturally into the correct position on your backhand, the lob is often easier to play on this flank. Reach
forward and get well down to the ball, because you have to

get your racket *under* it. There is hardly any backswing: just a flick of the wrist. As with the reverse angle and cross-court drop shot, your shoulders (on impact) will be parallel with the side wall. Stroke the ball upwards *before* it comes between your body and the side wall. Your face will be turned towards the nearest front corner. The ball is not so much hit as lifted. Swing so that the ball is already rising as it leaves the racket: it is important that the ball gains height early in its flight. It should strike well up the front wall and then, as it drops towards the back of the court, brush the side wall. If you stroke the ball too hard you will lift it out of court, or it will bounce well into court off the back wall. Your opponent will be grateful for either contingency. If you do not hit hard enough, or fail to gain that early height, then your opponent—again grateful, but unwilling to waste time on a speech of thanks—will clout the ball for a winner before you can turn round. So the lob has to be carefully played to achieve the height and length that are vital. But it is such a useful shot, with such a wealth of tactical advantages, that you cannot do without it. So master it as quickly as you can.

Spin

Squash is basically such a fast game that the deliberate application of spin is a risky business. The chances of error are increased because less of the racket face than usual is presented to the ball. So timing and touch must be fault-less. It follows that the golden rules governing the use of spin are: not too often, and not too much. Now that you have been warned, we have to add that the possibilities of spin cannot be ignored if your technique is to have the rich variety it will eventually need. Obviously there is a good deal of scope for spinning the ball by varying the swing, the angle of the racket face, and the use of the wrist. Top spin is not used in squash except for a few half-volleys, so the only kinds of spin we need to discuss here are cut and slice.

Cut

Cut is a natural—as distinct from a deliberate—spin. Because in squash, as you already know, most strokes are played with the head (or face) of the racket "open"—that is, with the head slanted so that the lower edge of the frame is nearer than the upper edge to the approaching ball. This inevitably applies a certain amount of the back spin known as cut, which tends to bring down the ball rather sharply after it has struck the front wall. The point of this is that the flight of the ball is checked, slightly but not completely, after the bounce. This in turn means that—assuming your shot has been well placed—your opponent will have to travel farther, faster, in order to make his return. All this concerns the moderate amount of cut applied to most of the strokes you play. We now move onto the deliberate application of increased cut—which you have probably seen used in both lawn tennis and table tennis when a player has to return a particularly powerful shot. It is also, of course, used in lawn tennis when volleying a fierce shot from the opponent, in order to bring the ball down just over the net (whereas a "flat" volley would put the ball yards out of court). In squash, this extra degree of cut demands that the face of the racket should be slightly more open than usual on the backswing, so that, on impact, the face is travelling both forwards and downwards. Let the swing and the angle of the racket face do the work—don't "chop" downwards as you would in table tennis, because this would drag the ball into the tin. You can use cut when serving, lobbing, or driving, to make the ball "stop" on a length instead of rebounding. You can use it on volleys and drop shots, to make the ball die in the nick. Whenever you want to kill the ball in the front of the court, you should use cut. You will probably find it easier to apply on the forehand than the backhand, unless you have an unusual wrist. You should never use it at all when playing a side wall shot, because the spin would bring the ball down into the tin.

As we have already said, your timing and touch must be faultless if deliberate cut is to be applied successfully. It follows that novices should not experiment with cut in match play. It needs a lot of practice (go to the front of the court for this, and hit the ball at the top of its bounce), because at first there will be a tendency to "lose" your normal swing and drag the ball down into the tin—or to get too far under the ball and hit it up to the ceiling. Remember that by reducing the amount of racket face presented to the ball, you are tampering with the orthodox and therefore taking a risk. So practise thoroughly. When the deliberate application of cut finally becomes a reliable part of your technique, so that it can be used with discretion in match play, there are two things to bear in mind: first, cut carries less risk when applied in the front half of the court (the only area from which you should attempt any sort of kill); second, the amount of cut you apply must be varied, or it will lose much of its element of surprise.

Slice

A right-hander, playing a forehand stroke, can put clockwise spin on the ball (anti-clockwise spin, if he is playing a backhand) by varying his swing so that the racket, as it travels forward across his body, is drawn in towards him. Slice cannot be applied when you have to stretch in order to reach the ball at all: because that forehand swing must start a little farther than usual from the right shoulder, curve in onto the normal path as it passes the body, and finish a little farther than usual from the left shoulder (during the follow-through, the racket head and the ball swerve away from you). The angle of the racket face has to be adjusted so that the face is turned towards the *side wall* on impact, dragging across the inside of the ball (the side nearest your body). Because of this unusual angle of the racket face, slice can only be applied with comfort and safety when the ball is below the level of the tin. This means in turn that the head of the racket has to be dropped almost as low as it is for the half-volley. The effect of all this is that the clockwise spin makes the ball shoot away to the right (on the forehand) at a greater angle than usual. So it would obviously be pointless to use slice when you are near to the side wall (equally, slice is far too risky to be used from the back of the court). Apply it only from the middle of the court, where it is both safe and effective.

Here, as with cut, you are tampering perilously with the orthodox, so slice must be practised carefully before you use it in match play. Remember that the work is done by adjustments in the swing and the angle of the racket face. Beware of putting too much slice on the ball. The spin makes the ball come off the front wall quite quickly and at a wide angle. It aims to make the ball die sooner, and farther away, than your opponent expects. But too much slice will make his job easier, because the ball will rebound off the side wall and come back into court, where he can play it without anxiety.

To sum up, both cut and slice are too useful to be neglected, but too difficult and dangerous to be used by novices in match play. You are playing with fire. If you must get your fingers burned, burn them in the privacy of your practice.

Return of Service

So far we have mainly been discussing technique, though we have tried to indicate the tactical uses of the various strokes. The task of receiving and returning service takes us into a field in which the emphasis is reversed. The strokes have already been examined. What you have to do now is to learn to "read" (i.e. anticipate) your opponent's game and take steps to deal with it. Receiving service is the obvious place to start, because unless you can do this competently, all your strokes will be useless and your opponent will have to do little more than bang over a succession of winning services. Happily, this sort of thing happens only to complete novices. You soon come to regard receiving service as just as much of an opportunity as a threat.

The most important thing is to get your "early warning system" organized. Primarily, this means watching the ball from the moment it leaves your opponent's hand. Many beginners make the mistake of watching the front wall instead—a mistake because this reduces the amount of time you have for reading the service and deciding what action to take. Besides watching the ball all the way, there are a few clues to help you to detect the type of service that is coming your way. If, for instance, your opponent stands at the front of the service box and drops his shoulder to serve, you can expect a lob: this will quickly be confirmed by the ball's sharp rise high onto the front wall. If a right-handed opponent serves backhand from the right-hand box, you can expect a service to a length, down the side wall and clinging to it. If he uses an overarm swing, he has violent intentions. This means you have to be mentally

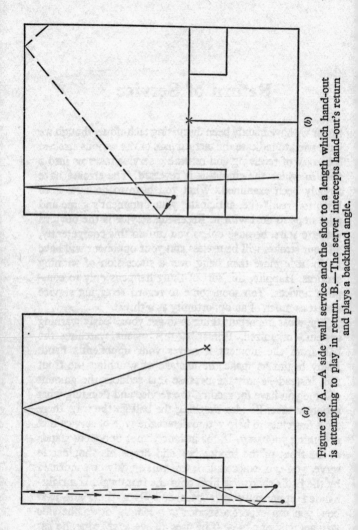

Figure 18 A.—A side wall service and the shot to a length which hand-out is attempting to play in return. B.—The server intercepts hand-out's return and plays a backhand angle.

and physically alert, ready to move fast. But you will have
a chance to seize the initiative, because as the ball cannons
round the back of the court, rebounding well clear of the
walls, there will be plenty of time for you to crack it as you
please . . . if you're sharp enough.

In addition to all this preliminary "reading", there are
several questions you have to answer, quickly, once the
service is on its way. Is the service bad enough to allow
you a straightforward volley? If so, play that way. Is the
ball going to hit the side wall? If it is, can you play a
volley *before* it does so? If you cannot volley before the ball
hits the side wall, will the ball rebound far enough off
the back wall to permit you a stroke? If not, volley the ball
as it comes off the side wall. Never strike at the ball as it hits
the side wall. Play it earlier or later. Make up your mind:
don't dither. If the ball is going to rebound helpfully
from the back wall, let it do so. Wait. Because this gives
you more time to prepare for a boast or a drive. Finally,
is the ball going to come off the side wall at such a sharp
angle that you will have to back away quickly (towards
the opposite back corner) in order to get a shot in?

All this is not as complicated as it may look at first sight.
Experience will soon teach you to ask the right questions
and find the right answers. All we have done is to show
you most of the examination paper in advance, to indicate
the lines on which you must think. Basically, your tasks
are these: 1, Watch the server; 2, Watch the ball; 3, Think
fast; 4, Make your decision; and 5, Get into position in
plenty of time. We cannot exaggerate the importance of
making up your mind fast and acting even faster. If you
can do this, you will give yourself the time you need to
make a decent return.

Your position of readiness is obviously important, since
you have to be prepared for anything. If your opponent
has any idea of the game, he will put most of his services
along that awkward line down the side wall, heading for the

back corner. So turn your body (not your head, because you are watching the server over your shoulder) towards the side wall. Stand about 4 ft. to 5 ft. from the half-court line and about a yard from the back wall. If your opponent is making effective use of a lob service, you will learn to move quickly towards the oncoming ball, so that you can go for an early volley. But don't move until your opponent has served, because if he spots you trying to "jump the gun" he will be crafty enough to vary his service accordingly. One last point about your position of readiness: your racket should rest lightly in the fingers of your "spare" hand (as in tennis) as your opponent prepares to serve. Immediately the ball is on its way, draw the racket partly back so that you swing smoothly into your stroke.

Right. You have done all you can in the way of preparation. Now for the actual return. Your basic aim, of course, is to play a shot that will shift your opponent from the mid-court position (he will be there a second after serving) and enable you to go there yourself. But do not try to play the ball direct onto the front wall unless you are sure you can manage it. Squash, like politics, is the art of the possible. You will probably have to be content with a defensive shot: if so, accept the fact and don't try to be clever. If your opponent is serving well, the volley is the shot you should go for, because a boast will leave your opponent in command at the front of the court. But the service may tamely invite you to make a choice from a selection of possible returns. We will list these in their order of usefulness.

First, a good length down (and close to) the nearest side wall. Second, a cross-court return high enough to elude your opponent's racket and hit the side wall, probably about 3 ft. below the out of court line and above the short line. Third, a lob to a length, either cross-court or down the nearest side wall. Fourth, a reverse angle. This surprise item is hit hard and low cross-court, onto the opposite side wall, rebounding towards the front corner on your

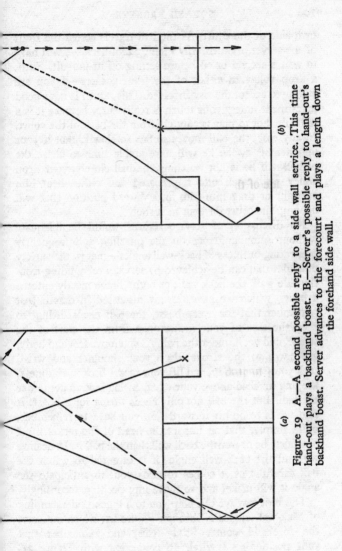

Figure 19   A.—A second possible reply to a side wall service. This time
hand-out plays a backhand boast. B.—Server's possible reply to hand-out's
backhand boast. Server advances to the forecourt and plays a length down
the forehand side wall.

(a)

(b)

own side of the court. As the ball travels across the front of the server, momentarily pinning him back, he will have to wait a second or so before setting off in pursuit. Fifth, a drop volley to either of the front corners—if you are willing to accept the risk involved. This return is not a good investment unless your touch is really sure, because it is a difficult shot to play accurately from the back of the court. In any case, the ball moves so far, so slowly, that if your opponent is awake he will have ample time to chase the ball. But if he is not watching the ball closely, your drop volley may catch him unprepared and either beat him outright or drag him into an awkward position that will open up the court for your next shot.

No discussion of service returns would be adequate without some guidance on the puzzling and frequently frustrating business of back-wall angles—that is, the variety of angles that can be achieved by services rebounding from the side wall, the back wall, or both. These mostly enforce a boast, which we have already discussed in detail. Just remember that for every boast, the ball needs lifting, so keep the face of your racket open from the start of the stroke, and get it under the ball. As you move feet and body, get down to the stroke, drop your shoulder and wrist, tuck your stomach in, and lift your racket back in readiness, keeping its head above your wrist. Swing low, to get under the ball. But the ball not only needs lifting for a boast: it also needs to be hit forwards. So you have to remember, quite simply, that on impact the head of the racket must obviously be nearer the back wall than the ball is. In dealing with all the back-wall angles it is essential to watch the ball carefully as it comes towards you, to anticipate the angle it will make, and to move into position accordingly.

The best way we can help you to a quick understanding of back-wall angles is through Figure 21, which indicates the forehand court. Study this, and remember that your positioning is vital. In connexion with Figure 21,

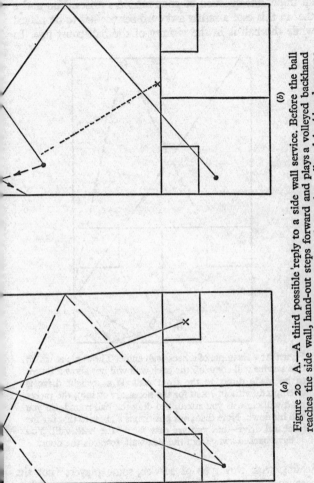

(a)

(b)

Figure 20 A.—A third possible reply to a side wall service. Before the ball reaches the side wall, hand-out steps forward and plays a volleyed backhand reverse angle. B.—Server's possible reply to the volleyed backhand reverse angle. Server advances to the forecourt and plays a backhand drop shot.

an important question of good manners arises. You notice that in this case a rather awkward service has to be played while the ball is in the vicinity of the half-court line. In

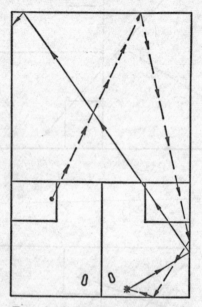

Figure 21 Example of a back-wall angle. The angle at which this service will come off the back wall will not allow a return to be made direct to the front wall. If a straight drive is attempted (without room for the necessary swing), the racket head will close as you attempt to drag the ball round. So you will hit down. Note that your position is similar to that for the forehand drive—but you are now facing the back wall. You have backed away from the side wall, towards the door.

dealing with this type of service, some players (not the best) turn round in order to hit the ball along the path it is already following. For example, they turn clockwise in the forehand court, in order to play a backhand. As they turn, they call "Turning!" to warn their opponent that they are about to hit the ball up *his* side of the court. This means the server has to take swift evasive action instead of occupying the mid-court position his good service should have earned him. If the player receiving service has to turn in this way, it means one of two things—he has either totally misjudged the flight of the ball and has therefore failed to position himself correctly, or he has no knowledge of the etiquette appropriate to the occasion. The accurate server should never be put at a disadvantage because of incompetence or bad manners on the part of the receiver.

Finally, a service will occasionally drop into the side wall or back wall nick. This is bad luck. You need fast reflexes to get such a shot back. A dead nick, which does not rise at all, is even worse luck, because you're done for. But no one can achieve a dead nick deliberately, and the law of averages makes it a rare event.

Match Play

We cannot play a match for you. But in previous chapters we have done all we can to help you in a technical sense. Now we move on to the fascinating field of strategy (pre-match planning) and tactics (adjusting your game to meet changing needs when you are in the middle of a match). The important thing is to be constructive, to think in positive terms, in order to get the fullest advantage from the equipment Nature has given you in the way of ability, physique, and sense. Make the most of what you have. All else being equal (and it frequently is), a match will be won and lost in the mind. The roll of champions—not only in squash, but in many other sports, too—is packed with the names of players who were certainly not the most talented of their day. They won because they had the wit and the courage to push their talents to the uttermost limits—this should be your aim, too, irrespective of your basic ability.

This chapter will help you. It cannot be absorbed at one reading. But browse through it. Take your time. Let your mind chew over the possibilities. There is much here that you will grasp immediately and put into practice. There is much else that will only strike home at a second or third reading. So come back to this chapter again and again as your game advances. When your technique has reached the limit of its possibilities, you can still improve—and keep on improving—as a match player. So use this chapter as an old friend, someone to whom you can always turn for advice, for a new slant on a problem that is bothering you.

It contains much that you have already absorbed. There

are a few little maxims that may help you towards positive thinking. Perhaps the most important is: Watch the ball. Here are a few more: Get to the middle of the court—but never put the ball there . . . Put the ball where your opponent will have maximum difficulty in retrieving it . . . Get your opponent in a corner—and the ball in the opposite corner . . . Try to hit to a better length than he does . . . Keep him behind you—because it's the man in front who hits the winners . . . Let him know what you are going to do—and then do something else . . . Keep moving—and keep thinking . . . Squash is chess speeded up—make your opponent the pawn . . . Run him into the ground—and then put the pressure on . . . But keep your head—accuracy is more important than violence . . . Don't change a winning game—but always change a losing game.

Obvious? May be. But that brings us to a last maxim: Never neglect the obvious.

Now for some more detailed advice.

Reconnaissance

There is a good deal that you can do before even hitting the ball. Later we will discuss ways of assessing your opponent from such evidence as his age, his physique, and what you know of his game. In addition, have a close look at the court and remember the notes we gave you in the chapter devoted to this. Note the height of the roof and the position of lights and girders, because all this will affect your use of the lob. Is it a warm or cold court? If it is warm, the ball will be lively, the rallies long, and you may have to work patiently for your openings before going for winners. If it is cold, the ball will die quickly—and drop shots, angles, lobs, and drives to a length will all pay quick dividends. If the court is sweating, it will be pointless to use angles or lobs, because the ball will just skid off the wall into trouble: all you can do is hit low and hard. You will learn to assess the speed of the ball, too. All these factors will help you to decide what sort of game to play, whether it will or will not be worth while to go for your winners.

One more point before you go into action: make sure that your shoelaces are securely tied, because if you have to interrupt the match in order to do them up, your rhythm and concentration will be broken.

The knock-up

Never mind whether the other chap makes good use of his five minutes or not. See that you do. The knock-up is too often casual. It shouldn't be, because you have a lot to do and not much time to do it in. This is your chance to get your eye in, to tune up body, footwork, and shots; to get your reflexes working, find your touch, and discover which of your shots are working well and which are not; to weigh up your opponent (his physical resources and the strengths and weaknesses of his technique); and, not least, to get to know the court and the way the ball is behaving. All this is a tall order for five minutes, especially as you have to make sure that your opponent has his fair share of practice: there are two men knocking up, remember, so don't hog the ball.

This is the only time errors cost you nothing. So go for your shots and try to get them all working smoothly. Move your feet, too. Use the knock-up to reacquire the habit of hitting your shots off the correct foot. Play backhands in the backhand court and forehands in the forehand court. This is another healthy habit, because if you play your shots in the wrong court during the match itself, you will have that much farther to travel in order to get back to midcourt.

Give your eyes and reflexes a chance to sharpen up. For a spell, stand in front of the short line, where the ball will be coming at you faster. After all, you intend to play the match from midcourt. So it would be silly to slip into slovenly ways by hanging back during the knock-up.

Do all this and you will be nicely loosened up and ready

to go. But do not ignore what your opponent is doing. Whether you know his game or not, the knock-up can give you an idea how his shots are working on that particular day. On the strength of all the knock-up evidence, as to his game and your own, you can then decide your strategy for the first game.

Begin at the beginning

The only time you can be sure of getting to midcourt first is when you are serving. Remember that at the beginning of each hand you can choose your service box. Do not keep serving first from the forehand box if you find that this is getting you nowhere—maybe your opponent is stronger on the backhand than the forehand. Or maybe you serve better to the forehand court. Find out.

Start with safe services, until you get into the swing of things. Then you can experiment a bit, with the various types of services, to discover how well or how badly your opponent copes with them. But when you have discovered which is your most effective service, it does not necessarily follow that you should use it all the time and risk "playing him in". If you can keep in front without it, that service may come in handy if and when you really need points. It's always comforting to have a trump card up your sleeve.

Central station

The only place from which you can maintain tactical command is midcourt, poised near the "T" formed by the junction of the short line and the half-court line. Go on court alone and stand there: see how much of the court you can cover by taking one stride and extending your racket. Remarkable, isn't it? Not much can elude you unless it is in a corner, too high to reach, or travelling fast close to a side wall. And even when the ball is in these awkward places, midcourt is still the best position to start from in covering all the possibilities. The lesson is plain enough. Move to midcourt, quickly, after every shot you play. (Don't make the common mistake of hanging farther back.) Once in midcourt, keep your opponent away from it—which means keeping the ball away from it. If you are in midcourt, your opponent must obviously be in one of the four quarters of the court. This gives you the straightforward tactical task of putting the ball in the diagonally opposite quarter, so that you can keep your opponent at full stretch. *Never* return the ball to midcourt. Put it in a corner, or close to the side walls. The point is that if you return the ball to midcourt you cannot go there yourself, because this would involve obstructing your opponent. And you *must* go to midcourt—so see that the ball does not.

If your opponent is in midcourt, you obviously have to play a shot that will shift him and enable you to take his place. The drop, the angle, the lob, and the clinger (especially when driven to a length) will all do the job. Should you play a shot that fails to move your opponent from midcourt, he may have the chance to play a winner.

So each rally becomes a battle for the midcourt position. Sooner or later one player will fail to draw his man away from it, and when that happens the end of the rally is near. If you find that your opponent is dominating the midcourt position in spite of all your efforts, it is no bad idea to cut out your cross-court drives and, instead, concentrate on hitting straight down the side walls, to a length. At all levels of the game, cross-court drives are used to excess: they are meat and drink to a good volleyer in midcourt.

Everything in its place

Assuming that a rally is nicely balanced, with each man in turn slipping in and out of the midcourt position, then the placing of your shots becomes more and more important. It is vital to get your man out of position if you are to make an opening for a winner. Let us remind you of some basic principles. One is to put the ball in the part of the court farthest from your opponent (or, if he's behind you, farthest from the place where you last saw him). The stroke you use for the purpose depends on personal choice or the circumstances of the moment, since there is usually more than one way of putting the ball in a particular place (for example, angle or cross-court drop, drive or lob). A second basic principle is this: if you see your opponent moving quickly, put the ball into the part of the court he's leaving . . . he will have very little time to change from forward into reverse gear, or vice versa.

There are a few more points that may help your tactical thinking when it comes to "picking your punches". For instance, by trying to be too clever you may make your opponent's task easier. If he is behind you when you play your shot, do not *assume* that he has moved since playing his own shot. Make *sure* he moves. Make him sweat. If he is in a back corner and expects you to make him run to the diagonally opposite front corner, why disappoint him? Whatever his expectations, he will not enjoy the long journey at full speed, especially if you keep on forcing him to make it. So insist that he goes. Do not play back to his original position unless you have strong evidence that he has gone somewhere else. Having made him move from A to B, *this* is the time to put the ball back to A again. (You may have to lob the ball over him in order to do this, if he is hanging about on the line from A to B.) All this is tough for the poor devil. But after all, you are playing to win. So never underrate the obvious. If you can keep up a pattern like this—A to B and back to A again—it will not be long before your opponent turns up late for his appointment with the ball.

As with the direction of your shots, so with the shots themselves. Don't try to be too clever. For example, why risk that difficult shot, the reverse angle, when the much safer drop shot will put the ball more accurately into exactly the same place? We are not telling you to do the obvious all the time. We *are* telling you to do the obvious *most* of the time. It is difficult enough, and very effective if you can maintain your shot-control.

A few more thoughts about this business of discretion as an aid to winning matches. If you try to kid yourself that things are better than they really are, they will probably get worse. Translated into practical squash, this means that you should not play attacking shots from defensive positions. Recognize the realities of every situation. Experience will soon teach you when an attacking shot is or is not "on". But you can give experience a nudge in the right direction by a little habit-forming exercise during the days when you are still tactically raw. For a few minutes, even for a whole match, tell yourself "Attack" or "Defend" after every shot your opponent plays. It is a question of assessing the shot he has played, the position you are in, and the possibilities open to you in those specific circumstances.

In general, defensive shots are mostly slow and high, to give you time. When receiving service, it is usually wise to play safe, to a length. Another situation demanding discretion arises when you have to deal with a high ball at the back of the court. Do not try to hit it low, for a winner. Play for length. Similarly, do not play a drop shot or angle when your opponent is in front of you—unless he is travelling fast towards the back of the court.

Make a firm mental note of the "accident zone"—the part of the court in which over-ambitious shots lead to a high proportion of errors. This zone extends, roughly, from 1 ft. to 6 ft. behind the short line. It is a zone, 5 ft. by 21 ft., which is a sort of no-man's-land between attack and defence, a zone in which you should always be conscious of the danger of throwing your weight about without good cause.

Finally, in the way of keeping everything in its place, maintain a sense of perspective about the scoring system.

When in hand, you can afford to take a few chances and go for your winners, because even if you come unstuck, all you lose is the service. But when you are hand-out, any mistake you make will cost you a point—so let your opponent take the risks. Similarly, you can obviously afford to take more chances when you have a useful lead: but don't let it go to your head. As we said before, don't change a winning game.

Strength to strength

Make the most of what you have, but do not assume that your "good" and "bad" shots are constant. One day your drop shots may be faultless. The next day you may be putting them down. This is something you can usually find out during the knock-up. Cut your coat according to your cloth. In squash, as in life as a whole, what was true yesterday is often false today.

If you discover that you have a particular shot that baffles your opponent, do not use it regularly unless you are in trouble. If you can stay ahead without that shot, why give your opponent the chance to get the hang of it? Save it: during a possible later crisis you will be glad to have such a weapon in reserve.

If you are fit, there should be no need to take risks. If you are unfit, then go for quick winners. If you and your opponent are equally fit, but you have the more positive game, go for winners. If your opponent has a greater flair for the game and is technically the better player, do not despair: you may still outwit him. Skill, wits, speed, fitness, "guts" . . . they all count, and a deficiency in one sphere may be made up in others. The finest stroke players in the game can be reduced to defeat, especially on warm courts, by men with more in the ways of wits, fitness, or determination. There is no substitute for hard work: physical, mental, and moral. As Edison put it, "Genius is one per cent inspiration and ninety-nine per cent perspiration."

How goes the enemy?

Have a look at the other chap. If he is tall, don't use the lob unless you have to, because he will probably be good overhead. You may find, too, that he has a long enough reach to intercept your cross-court drives. But he may have trouble bending, or turning quickly. Find out. If he is short, he may be quick about the court, but is probably vulnerable to the lob. If he is fat, he may give the ball a fair old clout, but his stamina will be suspect and probably his speed too (though fat people are often quite nimble over a yard or two). He will certainly not enjoy a lot of twisting and bending. If he is old, he is probably experienced, so it will be a good idea to keep him away from the front of the court —where he could probably show you a thing or two. So pin him back and tire him out.

Now for his game. Find out his strengths and weaknesses. Starve his strong shots. Feed his weak ones. To put it another way, find out what he likes, and don't give it to him: find out what he doesn't like, and give it to him. Does he like a fast game or a slow one? Whatever game he plays well, disrupt it. If he likes the back of the court, driving to a length, use your short game to send him scuttling up to the front wall. If he is hot stuff with drop shots and angles, hold him back with drives and lobs, and avoid shots that will bring him forward—unless you are sure you have built up the ideal position for a winner. Hit hard, to knock his delicate little game for six. If a particular shot keeps letting him down, make him play it. If he is fit and fast, your drop shots may be ineffective and you may find that the only way to beat him is by deception, by making him run the wrong way. Just because you cannot beat his fitness, it does not follow that you cannot beat his brain.

But if you do succeed in getting him tired, break his stamina and morale altogether by increasing the pace and lengthening the rallies a little, instead of going for quick but risky winners (you might hit a few down, and in any case short rallies would help him to get his breath back).

One final thought on adjusting your game to make things as awkward as possible for your opponent. Remember that the type of game you like least may be even less to the liking of your opponent; conversely, that he may be even better than you are at the type of game you prefer. So keep an open mind. Watch him. The knock-up should give you a few clues and the first game should supply most of the answers.

He who runs may read

"Reading" a rally is the craft of anticipation, of knowing in advance the problems your opponent is about to set you. Experience is a great teacher in this field, but there are a few elementary principles you can apply right away: Watch the ball . . . Watch your opponent, especially his racket and his wrist . . . From the position he is in, ask yourself what he can do . . . Be ready to move fast in exploiting the information you have. Do all this and you will continually be starting so soon, and covering the court so smoothly, that your opponent will begin to suspect you have a sixth sense that takes you to the right place at the right time.

To read a rally well is to concentrate constructively, and this is a process that should go on for every second the ball is on the move. Only for the few seconds between rallies, and the minute between games, can you allow your concentration to relax—and even then you should be thinking over the way things are going, and asking yourself whether any adjustments are needed in your strategy. Do not let your concentration slacken just because things are going well: your opponent may be a slow starter, or may be on the point of changing his own strategy.

Concentration is easier in the confined space of a squash court than it is on "open" courts (for example, lawn tennis

courts), where there are more visible distractions. The
trouble with squash is the tendency to become almost
mesmerized by following the flight of the ball for rally
after rally, game after game. This mesmeric effect is exaggerated by tiredness. But fight it. Your concentration must
always be constructive. At the end of a long, close, and
gruelling match, it is the man who has retained the power
of positive thinking who wins.

Pianoforte

A common enough word which, in its literal sense of "soft-
loud", marries music with the tactical demands of most
ball games. We often hear of otherwise gifted sportsmen
dismissed as "one-pace" players. In squash, as in other
games, they are relatively easy to beat because you can upset
their rhythm by changes of pace, whereas they cannot do
the same to you. Once you have absorbed the rhythm of their
game, there is nothing—in the way of quickening or slowing the pace—that they can do to upset you. So make sure
that, from the very beginning of your career, you keep
adjusting the pace of *your* shots. It should be part of the
normal tactical pattern of your game to vary the pace
continually in an effort to enforce error. There is no point
in hitting hard all the time: it is a waste of energy that
you may need later.

There will be many occasions when you need to increase
or reduce the pace deliberately, because of tactical con-
siderations. Obvious examples are slowing the game down
when you are tired, or when your opponent is hustling you
into error, and quickening the pace in order to put pressure
on when you have taken over the midcourt position, or
when your opponent is tiring.

To reduce the pace, take the ball later, after the top of
the bounce and farther back in the court. Volley less. Lob
more. Slow down the head of the racket at the moment of
impact. Stroke the ball rather than hit it. To increase the

pace, take the ball earlier, which means making intercep-
tions at the front of the court and volleying as often as
possible. Or hit the ball before the top of the bounce. Use
hard hitting, to a length, mixed with drop shots. Increase
the speed of the racket head (except on drop shots, of
course) so that you punch through the ball on impact.
Remember that violence alone does not increase the pressure, since your opponent will be able to stay at the back
of the court: short balls are just as important if you are to
make him cover the maximum distance in the minimum
time.

Intent to deceive

As we have said, there are times in squash when, all else
being equal, you have to turn to deception as the basis of
success. The idea is to keep your opponent on the hop, in a
constant state of dithering uncertainty about your intentions. For instance, you can lull him into a false sense of
security by repeatedly playing a particular stroke from a
particular position—and then suddenly doing something
different. After that, he will never be sure. For example,
get him in a back-court routine and then play a drop, or
an angle, or a hard, low hit aimed for the nick in the front
half of the court. Similarly, you can play a drive or lob
when you have led him to expect a drop—or you can play a
drop when you have led him to expect a drive or lob.
Another variant is the angle, when he is expecting a drop,
a drive, or a lob. The variations are many. From either of
the two front quarters of the court, remember, all the four
basic shots are "on"—drive, drop, angle, and lob. Assuming
that you can play all four of them accurately, their efficiency
will depend on the sense with which you mix them up.

Your stance and swing can both be varied, as an added
means of deception, once your game begins to progress.
The most obvious example probably occurs when you take
a long swing as you dash towards one of the front corners,

but then—at the last moment—check that swing, steady yourself, and play a drop shot. In the same way you may set yourself up for a drop shot—and then punch the ball to a length with a whip of the wrist.

This brings us to the most subtle form of deception, masking—an art in which the Egyptian players have always excelled. What this involves is a sudden turn of the wrist at the moment of impact, to produce a stroke your opponent does not expect—with the aim of catching him on the wrong foot, or moving the wrong way. This sort of trickery is at its most effective when you are up near the front wall. But it requires a good wrist and a sure touch. Novices may find that in match play (as opposed to practice) it does their cause more harm than good. So be sparing with your attempts at masking, until you have learned to do all the simple things well.

Never turn your back

When drawn to the front of the court, play your shot and then *back* towards midcourt—on such a line that you will not impede your opponent. Never turn your back on the front wall. If you do, you might as well sit down and have a breather for all the chance you will have of staying in the rally. Have you ever seen a goalkeeper turn his back on a shot? Or a wicketkeeper crouching at the stumps with his back to the bowler? You are in a similar situation: the ball (which, over your shoulder, you are watching your opponent hit) is about to come your way pretty fast off the front wall. So if you turn your back on the front wall you don't need a coach . . . you need a psychiatrist.

The con man

Like most games, squash has its share of confidence tricksters. They work in three phases—dressing room, knock-up, and match. There are two basic tricks: one is to kid you that you haven't got a chance; the other is to kid you that *he* hasn't. During phase one, in the dressing room, he may tell you that he is fitter than he has ever been ... or that he feels ill. He may tell you that he has had a lot of squash lately and is playing better than ever ... or that it is ages since he played last, so that he's very rusty. He may tell you that he has always had a wonderful flair for the game, and give you a list of his big wins ... or that he has always been a mug, and never beats anyone with two sound legs. He may tell you that he has a superb drop shot (when in fact it's useless) ... or that he has no backhand (when in fact it's his best shot). He may flex his muscles like a he-man and do a few brisk press-ups to frighten you ... or start slapping his legs and complaining of pulled muscles or recent injuries.

Listen politely, but let it all go in one ear and out of the other.

The same process, slightly adjusted, will continue during the knock-up—slightly adjusted because pretence becomes more difficult once the ball is flying about. But he will still try to "con" you into getting false ideas about his game and his physical resources. The match itself takes him into phase three. He may begin to look exhausted and distressed between rallies, and underline the implications with such comments as "I'm whacked", "That's me finished", or "I'm getting too old for this game". Or he may hit a few good but (unknown to you) lucky shots and say "I'm in great shape today", "I'm going like a bomb—it looks as though your luck's out", or "It's a long time since I've played so well and felt so fit—still as fresh as a daisy".

Don't believe him. Stick to the evidence of your own eyes. His speed and stamina during the rallies themselves (as distinct from his behaviour between them) are your only sure guides to his condition. To sum up, never accept anything such an opponent tells you—or implies by his physical reactions—before or during a match. It is all part of the act. Find out the truth without his "help". Just as important, never give a thing away yourself: never reveal surprise, dissatisfaction, or fatigue. Keep him guessing.

There are, of course, other ways of trying to "con" you out of a match. For instance, "delaying tactics" are commonly used by unscrupulous players who want to break your concentration or make you irritable (both, if they can manage it). They can keep you waiting by taking a long time over the service—or, when you are serving, by pretending they are not ready. Between rallies they can knock the ball up the court and stroll slowly after it; or beg time so that they can fetch a handkerchief; or leave the court for no reason at all. A player who wears glasses may stop too often, for too long, in order to wipe them with excessive care. The shoelace dodge is also popular—for no good reason, your opponent suddenly decides that his laces need untying and retying. These are just a few of the "con" man's tricks. Look out for them, and others. Keep calm, and concentrate on the match, not the diversions. Now that you have been warned in advance, you should never be "conned".

The inquest

Just as important as assessing an opponent before you play him (and in this respect it's a good idea to watch him play somebody else, if you have the chance) is the inquest afterwards. Because in squash, as in life, "you can't win them all'. What you can do is avoid making the same mistakes twice. After a defeat, just remember that you play as well as your opponent allows you to play. If you played badly, why did it happen? If he was hitting winners, what sort of game would have denied him the opportunities? If you were making a lot of mistakes, was this because of your own poor concentration, or because you were being hustled or tricked into them? What sort of game did your opponent play—was he going for his shots, hitting hard, or using the lob to keep things going steadily while you made the mistakes? Work it all out. Never let the same opponent beat you again with the same game. Recognize the sort of game that doesn't suit you, and devise means of thwarting it. Once again we are back to the importance of positive thinking—which can kindle the flame of future victory from the ashes of present defeat.

Etiquette

"Whatsoever ye would that men should do to you, do ye even so to them." Make this your text for the game: and repress the cynicism that may tempt you, in a moment of mischief, to paraphrase it as: "Do him before he does you." Squash provides unparalleled opportunities for being nasty. Consider the situation . . . two men, both brandishing rackets, hurtling about a confined space at high speed. The imagination boggles at the possibilities for carnage. There is clearly unusual scope for the unscrupulous. But in squash there are not many of them about. Keep it that way. The game is made or marred by the manners of the people playing it, and your behaviour should be exactly the same as the behaviour you expect from your opponent. In the peculiar conditions of the game, a passive sense of decency is not enough: squash demands a *positive effort* to be fair. Now let us progress from the general to the particular . . .

Wear white, so that your opponent has no difficulty in following the flight of the black ball. Make sure that all your clothes, especially your shoelaces, are secure: otherwise you may have to interrupt the play, and keep your opponent waiting, while you make the necessary adjustments. During the knock-up, give your opponent a fair share of the ball and hit it to him in such a way that he can play a proper stroke, instead of having to pick it up off the floor. Practice an occasional angle or drop shot by all means, but don't hog the ball for more than three consecutive strokes. Watch your backswing and follow-through, and keep your wrist flexible. Because the big swing and locked wrist of lawn tennis are highly dangerous if used in squash

(in which both players are on the same side of the "net").
Before and during the match, never be guilty of any of the
sharp practices we listed under "The Con Man" in our
chapter on "Match Play". Make a close study of rules 14,
17, 21, and 24. If you get the chance before or after your own
match, have a crack at marking or refereeing another match:
this will teach you a lot about the game and make you feel
at home with the rules.

When getting to midcourt, never obstruct your opponent,
cramp his stroke, or interfere with him in any way. There
are two similar situations in which you should be particularly careful: when playing a drop shot, or when tucked
in one of the back corners taking part in an exchange of
length driving up and down the same side wall. On neither
occasion should you return to midcourt on a straight line.
Each time your first move should be towards the opposite
side wall, to leave your opponent with a clear run to the ball.
Having made that first move, you can then get back to midcourt as fast as you like. To illustrate the point by examples,
after playing a drop shot to the right-hand corner, your
first move should be to the left; similarly, after digging
your return out of the right-hand corner, and playing the
ball back to the same place, your first move should again
be to the left. This means that in all such cases your recovery to midcourt follows a curving course, rather than
a straight line.

The drop shot often produces an unfortunate tendency
for its exponent to stand and admire the delicacy of his art—
unmindful of the unseen opponent who is charging towards
him like a giant greyhound. Two things can happen—
either the drop shot specialist is suddenly smashed in the
back by what feels like a runaway train (and be aggrieved
about it); or the opponent puts all his brakes on, stops in
time, and is awarded at least a let, and possibly the rally.
There is no harm in shielding the ball from your opponent
while you are actually playing your drop shot—but you

must not hang about for even a second after impact. Get out of the way. Fast. If the position is reversed, and your opponent hangs about after playing a drop shot, *never* charge him in the back. Ask for a let.

With the best will in the world, two players may, at times, get in each other's way and occasionally collide. In these cases, apologize immediately if you are at fault—and ask for a let if the other chap is. But if, by a bad return or faulty positioning, you yourself create a situation in which you have to ask for a let, it will not be granted. Nor will you be awarded a let if the referee considers that you could not have got to the ball in time anyway, or that your opponent's shot was a winner. Always ask for a let with courtesy and show the same courtesy in accepting the decision. These situations crop up in squash: lets are part of the game, and referees and markers are there to see fair play. (If there is no official in charge, and your opponent is being naughty, keep your temper—and insist on asking your opponent for a let whenever you think it justified.) When you are denied a fair view of the ball, or a free run to it, or your opponent is hampering your swing and forcing you to play a cramped stroke, or is likely to be endangered by your stroke, do not swing—ask for a let. Do your best to ensure that your opponent never has similar grounds for asking for a let. If you mishit the ball, be especially alert in nipping out of the way—because a mishit means the ball is not going where you wanted it to, and you may be in the way as a consequence. But although your courtesy should be unfailing, it should not be excessive: don't handicap yourself by creeping quietly into a corner and giving your opponent an open court to play in. Be fair—but don't be daft.

There are times when your opponent will be between you and the front wall. If you hit him with the ball when it would otherwise have gone direct onto the front wall, you win the rally. If the ball was going to hit a side wall before reaching the front wall, you get a let. It is debatable

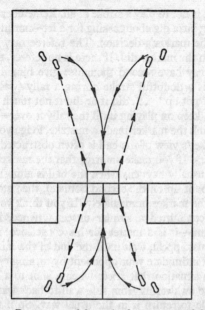

Figure 22   Routes to and from the four corners of the court.
This illustrates, first, the way you should be free to approach
the corners—and the care with which you should leave the
same routes clear for your opponent when he is on the same
errands. Second, it shows your route back to midcourt—a
route that avoids obstructing your opponent. If you do not
get out of the way, quickly, on the recovery route shown, you
will concede lets or (worse) penalty points. So the recovery
route is not just good manners: it is the only sensible and legal
way of getting back to midcourt. When beginning this return
journey, push off from the foot nearest the side wall (assuming
you were correctly positioned for your stroke). Always face
the front wall during your return journey.

whether you should ever hit your opponent in such a situation. Certainly there is never any excuse for hitting him
hard—and if you risk trying to play the ball gently onto
his back, you may miss, and thus lose the rally. So your

safest bet is not to play a stroke at all. Remember that there is nothing infra dig about asking for a let—nor in appealing against the marker's decision. The referee may have seen more than the marker did. If there is no referee, the marker himself may have second thoughts: give him the chance. If there is a doubtful stroke during a rally (was that shot "up" or "not up" ... did it or did it not touch the top of the tin?), keep on playing until the rally is over—and then, if you think the marker made a mistake, lodge your appeal. The marker's view of the ball is often obstructed by one of the players. If you make an error that the marker does not see (this usually happens when the ball is almost dead and you scrape it up on the second bounce), then stop playing and tell the marker immediately. If you think your opponent has committed a similar unseen offence, keep your mouth shut—it is a matter for his conscience, not yours. If you must appeal, wait until the end of the rally.

Do not intimidate your opponent by turning on the ball. This is a situation that arises when a shot to a length rebounds so awkwardly from side wall to back wall that you are unable to return it in the usual way. So if the ball is humming down your backhand, you turn round to follow the ball and, after it has rebounded from the back wall, play a forehand stroke up the right-hand side of the court. This is bad manners, even though you may warn your opponent with the cry "Turning!" Because it means that his shot has been too good for you—and that in order to get it back you are putting him under the positional handicap of having to duck, or take other evasive action. This would never occur if you played a correct return before your opponent's shot travelled far enough to embarrass you.

Finally, keep your temper, whatever happens. The man who cannot control himself is hardly likely to control a match.

Look and Learn

You can read about the game and talk about it. You can train and you can practise. You can take lessons and you can play matches. But in the midst of all this, never forget the value of watching the best players in action. After all, if a game is worth playing at all it is worth playing well—and the men and women who already play well can obviously do a lot to get your mind working on the right lines. The peak months of the British season are from December to March inclusive. The men's open and amateur championships are usually held in December and January respectively, the women's championship in February. These events are all played on the warm courts of London's West End clubs (and by now you are well aware of the strenuous, inhibited type of game that a warm court demands). Next in importance on the fixture list are the international matches, usually played in the capital cities of the four home countries. Lower down the scale, there is plenty of high class competition all over the country. Watch the best if you can—and do not watch casually. Use your intelligence to analyse what is going on.

You will quickly notice several basic points—the close attention with which the players watch the ball and each other; their quickness in getting the racket back early before they play their strokes; their instinctive movement towards the vital midcourt position after playing a shot; and their persistence in hitting to a length. Look out for the player whose easy, flowing style attracts you and might be worth imitating. The striker will always be chasing the ball, so pay particular attention to the non-striker—his positioning, his watchfulness, his anticipation. Note the type of game each man is playing (fast or slow?) and break it down into its component parts. What shot is he using to draw his man up the court: drop shot or angle? See how the pace changes during a rally, or is suddenly varied by one player when things are going badly for him. If he starts using a lot of lobs it may mean that he is trying to slow down a game that is being played too fast for him—or that he is tired, and needs a breather. The better player, you observe, is always watching the ball and his opponent's racket, and moving into position with time to spare. The other chap may be hurrying and stretching and lunging. Try to spot the moment in a rally when one man suddenly gains the initiative. The decisive shot is not always the last. It could come several strokes earlier, with a shot that breaks up the pattern of a rally and puts one man in charge and the other on a string. Watch the pressure build up from that moment, and see whether the man in charge presses his advantage home, or loses it.

Each man in turn will keep trying to deceive his opponent, and sooner or later one of them will be caught napping. Then his opponent will step up the pace by taking the ball earlier and volleying more. Watch where they put the ball, and ask yourself why. Try to anticipate, from your own knowledge of the game, what should happen next—and see if it does. You can even make a note of the decisive shots, both good and bad, and thus work out the technical strengths and weaknesses of each man on court. One may put a lot of his backhand drop shots into the tin. Another may hit several winners with his forehand angle. The players themselves (those watching, as well as those on court) are quick to spot these things. At the beginning of each rally, notice the type of service used and the box from which it is played. Does it give the server the initiative or not—and why? Look at the receiver, where and how he stands. Watch whether the service makes him play a defensive shot, or gives him a chance to attack. When lets are awarded, try to work out what happened that should not have happened —or what should have happened that did not happen.

Listen to all the chat that is going on around you, because much of it will be well informed. If you happen to be near a good player you know, encourage him to talk about the match. Squash players are usually great enthusiasts and will discuss the game for hours if they get the chance. If you are lucky enough to know a professional, let him talk about the game for as long as he's prepared to.

If you can cram all this into a night out at one of the big championships, your thinking about the game will be stimulated, enriched, expanded. You will be full of new ideas. The following morning, look at the paper—*The Times*, *The Guardian*, and *The Daily Telegraph* all report the major championships. There may be a sentence here and there that tells you something you have missed, or throws a new light on some aspect of the play.

To sum up: look, listen, and learn today—and you will be a better player tomorrow.

Fitness and Practice

Exercise is good for us. On a squash court, it's fun, too. Our primitive ancestors kept bodies and minds in trim by trying to stay alive, which was not easy in the old days. Even now, the young are naturally fit. But once we are old enough to earn a living, the daily grind encourages physical decline. There's always something to worry about, always another job waiting to be done. We spend far too much time sitting down—at a desk, at the wheel of a car, in an armchair. With our bodies regularly at rest, fat accumulates, the circulation worsens, and all our physical resources are weakened by disuse. We become easy prey for all sorts of ills—and a sluggish body leads to a sluggish mind. It is, of course, a help to do some deep breathing—in through the nose and out through the mouth—in front of an open window when we get up in the morning. Nor should "physical jerks" be despised. But exercise is the best preventive medicine—and for a busy man, squash is the best exercise. Circulation, respiration, muscles, eyes, reflexes—all are stimulated. *Mens sana in corpore sano* (a sound mind in a healthy body) becomes a reality again, just as it was at school. And with sound health, both physical and mental, we can bring vitality and enthusiasm to all we do in our everyday lives. Moreover, squash is as good a way as any of refreshing our minds by "getting away from it all".

For those of us past the first flush of youth, it is important to adapt the amount and the intensity of our endeavours to our physical condition—in other words, not to overdo it. Competitive squash can be harmful and possibly dangerous if its demands exceed our resources. The game allows none of the respites we get in lawn tennis—in squash, we're always on the go. So we have to be fit. For youngsters, this is no problem. They can play hard every day without ill effects. But the older we get, the more essential it is to have *regular* exercise—and at our own pace. From the middle thirties onwards we need habitual doses of fresh air and moderate exercise to keep us physically and mentally alert. But if middle-aged or elderly, we should resist the temptation to take on young opponents and try to play them at *their* pace. Remember, too, that the older we are, the more careful we have to be when resuming exercise after being out of action for a time: it is a question of taking things quietly for a few weeks and giving our bodies time to tune up again. Eventually, of course, advancing years will bring a day when even the gentlest of matches makes us feel thoroughly distressed —that will be the time to chuck squash in favour of something less strenuous. It's all a matter of common sense—of accepting physical resources as they are, instead of kidding ourselves that youth and fitness are permanent. The body is like a motor car—it will not look after itself. And even with the best care, the engine will eventually wear out.

But let us assume, for the moment, that you are still reasonably young and reasonably fit. To keep in good condition the old, golden rule is still the best—moderation in all things. A sound diet is important. This does not mean starving: merely being sensible about the quantity and the type of food you eat. As for smoking, and drinking alcohol, you will be fitter without them. Tobacco is the most harmful of the two. If you must smoke and drink, do so temperately. And if you are playing squash to lose weight, remember that a match will fail in its object if you sink a pint immediately afterwards!

Different games demand different types of fitness, because the stress comes on different muscles. You will soon find this out—if you have not already done so—when you switch between squash and, for example, lawn tennis or football. Once you have trained your body to the requisite standard of fitness at the beginning of each season, the best way to keep fit for playing squash is, quite simply, by playing squash. If you are going to play highly competitive squash, mental fitness is just as important as physical fitness. Many of the finest match players in squash—indeed, in all sports—make deliberate plans for getting their minds off the game until shortly before a big match, thus ensuring that they are mentally fresh and relaxed, instead of using up their reserves of nervous energy, and sapping their concentration, by worrying in advance. Jonah Barrington did this before depriving Abou Taleb of the open championship which the Egyptian had won for three successive years. Before the match, Richard Boddington, an experienced British international, took Barrington out in a car for an hour or so. They drove round the West End, had a look at the Christmas lights, and chatted about all sorts of things. When Barrington got to the dressing room he was relaxed, all anxiety and introspection gone. Aftab Jawaid of Pakistan, amateur champion for three successive years, was another expert in pre-match relaxation. Before a big match, he often had a quiet day out with friends, perhaps seeing something of the English countryside: always, the talk was of anything except squash. Small wonder that he tended to sleep well on the eve of the match. The amount of time spent in bed on these occasions is less important than how *well* you sleep. There is no point in going to bed at 10 o'clock if you can't sleep because of worrying about the coming match and your opponent. It's better to have a carefree day, get to bed at midnight, and sleep soundly. Another useful aid in saving all your nervous energy for the match is to give yourself ample time to get to the courts—don't set off late and have a nerve-wracking rush. Set off early, take your time, and do everything slowly until you actually get on court.

This problem of relaxation is, of course, mainly for the

advanced player rather than the beginner. But at all levels, physical preparation is vital. Barrington's historic "double" in the open and amateur championships of 1966–67 was based not on his superior squash, but on his superior

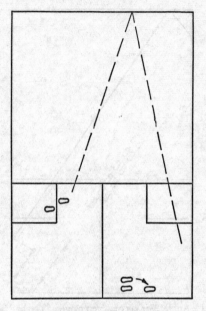

Figure 23   Service and return. For two players. One serves, and the other stands prepared to play a return.

physical condition. Besides his skill and his tactical maturity, he had the capacity to "pace" a match and, eventually, run his opponents into the ground. He had devoted himself 100 per cent to the task of winning—and there are few people, in any sport, who have the strength of character to work as hard as he did. If you are one of those who think no game is worth dedicated, disciplined preparation of strokes, tactics, and body, if you cannot practice moderation in eating, drinking, and smoking, then you must not expect to play really well or get far in high class competition. Because there is no room for "playboys" in top squash. But

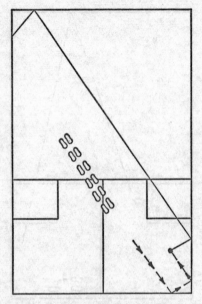

Figure 24   Angle. For six or seven players. The ball is thrown into the corner (→ →) and each player in turn practises an angle.

if you *are* prepared to work, then there are several rather obvious off-court exercises for getting in trim. Road work is one—a daily jog in the fresh air. Skipping is useful, too, since it brings all the muscles into play and encourages quick footwork. Weight training (under proper supervision) will also build up strength where you need it. Or "developers" may help to improve wrists, arms, shoulders, and back. Running and skipping are, of course, general exercises. The others are specific—applied to particular muscles. The sort of work you do obviously depends on your personal physical weaknesses. All this is not to say

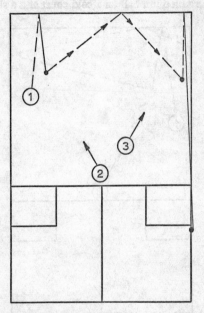

Figure 25   For three players. 1 "feeds" a short ball to 2, who advances from midcourt and attempts to play a backhand cross-court nick. 3 advances from midcourt and—unless the ball is a dead nick—tries to hit it to a length.

that you have to train like a Barrington in order to enjoy your squash: we are merely pointing out the sort of sacrifices you will have to make if you intend to make your mark at the *highest* level of the game. Whatever your ambitions, never overdo the training—it should not outlast your zest for it.

We have indicated the importance of physical and mental fitness and given you a few ideas about training. So you know how to get in trim for the game. Now we turn to on-court preparation: in other words, practice. Here, as in competition, use a medium ball on a cold court and a slow ball on

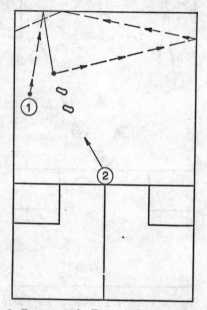

Figure 26   Reverse angle. For two players. 1 "feeds" a short ball to 2, who advances from midcourt and (note the position of the feet) plays a backhand reverse angle.

a warm court. Given two players similarly fit and well trained, similarly determined, and similarly shrewd in their tactical knowledge, then the better stroke player—the man with the more consistent control over the ball—will win. This is why your practice is so important. It gives you the chance to get your stance, footwork, and strokes properly organized, so that—thoroughly well drilled—you play your strokes *instinctively* in match play. Instinct is the reaction born of experience, and your chances in match play depend on the correctness of that reaction. Because in competition you have no time to analyse each stroke before

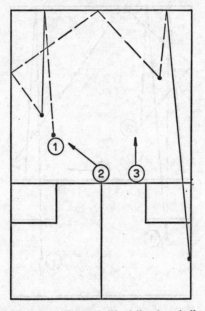

Figure 27   For three players. 1 "feeds" a short ball to 2, who advances from midcourt to play a backhand angle. 3 then advances from midcourt to hit this to a length.

you play it. All you can hope is that your strokes have been properly groomed in practice.

We are not going to insist that one form of practice is better than another. Practising alone, for instance, has much to commend it, though it can obviously be of little help to you in a tactical sense. Alone, you can work on individual shots until you get them right. You can also play 'rallies" that will improve your ball control and your movement about the court. This will soon teach you that you will not hit the ball in the direction you want unless your feet are properly positioned. You can work out your own sequences

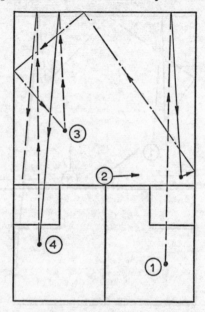

Figure 28 For 4 players. 1 tries to hit to a length. 2 steps across from midcourt to intercept and play an angle. 3 and 4 both try to hit to a length

of strokes for these rallies. For example—a backhand cross-court lob, then a forehand boast, followed by a backhand drop shot and, finally, a length down the backhand wall. Or a backhand angle, then a forehand drop, a forehand cross-court lob, a backhand boast and, finally, a length down the forehand wall. These little rallies will do your ball control and fitness a lot of good. At first you will have to go through the routines gently, hitting the ball fairly high. But as your accuracy and quickness improve, you will be able to hit the ball harder and lower. In devising your own rallies, be sure to bring in the four basic strokes—drive, drop, lob, and angle or boast. Another popular and highly useful form of solo practice is to stand in the centre of the court, two or three yards from the front wall, and play a mixture of angles and drops to each front corner in turn, never letting the ball bounce more than once. Keep the "rally" going as long as possible. This, again, will do much for your ball control and footwork. Hit the ball gently at first, and well above the tin. Then, as we said before, hit harder and lower as you improve.

Practising in pairs extends your range and means you can now simulate match conditions, besides working on individual strokes. Player A may practise lobs and drives while player B retrieves from the back corners. Each should acquire the healthy habit of nipping back to midcourt after every shot. One or the other can go for a winner after a while—a prospect that will keep each man mentally alert. Another routine is for player A to practise nothing but defensive shots to a length down the side wall, while player B goes for any shot he fancies. Try this for a complete game—then change roles for a second game. In addition to its basic value for improving ball control and footwork, this routine will give each man good tactical experience, since in match conditions he will have to play—and combat—each type of game. As for the "short game", you can practise this by playing a game in front of the short line, using nothing but angles, reverse angles, and drops. This will do your reflexes a lot of good—and teach you to keep out of your opponent's way. A variant is for one man to play any strokes he chooses, while the other confines himself to drops and side-wall strokes.

The possibilities, as you see, are almost endless. And we

hope it is now clear that practice, that vital preparation for match play, can be fun rather than drudgery. Never practise at a standstill: move about, as you would during a match. And don't go on too long—stop when your physical or mental zest has evaporated. As for friendly practice matches, play all sorts of people in all sorts of conditions. Variety keeps you fresh, widens your experience, and makes you adaptable. Practise with better players as often as you can—though they should not be so much better that they beat you 9–0, 9–0, 9–0 every time. This will do your game no good at all. You are not going to improve your squash 100 per cent in a day. Your aim should be to make continual small improvements. No one ever climbed Everest in a hurry.

Useful Information

SECRETARIES' ADDRESSES

INTERNATIONAL SQUASH RACKETS FEDERATION.—
J. H. Horry, Squash Rackets Association, 26 Park
Crescent, London W.1.

Founder Members of I.S.R.F.

AUSTRALIA (Squash Rackets Association of Australia).—
K. W. Davenport, 20 Larool Avenue, Lindfield, New
South Wales.

GREAT BRITAIN (Squash Rackets Association).—J. H.
Horry, 26 Park Crescent, London W.1.

INDIA (Squash Rackets Association of India).—A. R. V.
Peermahomed, P.O. Box 930, Bombay.

NEW ZEALAND (New Zealand Squash Rackets Association).
—R. O. Haddon, P.O. Box 86, Palmerston North.

PAKISTAN (Pakistan Squash Rackets Association).—
Lieut.-Cmdr. A. Rashid, P.N., Naval Headquarters,
Karachi.

SOUTH AFRICA (Squash Rackets Association of Southern
Africa).—H. Bilbrough, P.O. Box 10972, Johannesburg.

UNITED ARAB REPUBLIC (United Arab Republic Squash
Rackets Association).—K. Zaghloul, Gezira Sporting
Club, Cairo.

Affiliated to S.R.A.

IRELAND.— B. W. T. McHugh, Fitzwilliam Lawn Tennis
Club, Wilton Place, Dublin 2.

ISLE OF MAN.—P. W. Dodsworth, The Villiers Hotel,
Douglas.

JERSEY.—J. A. Queree, Mayfair Hotel, St. Saviour's Road, Jersey, Channel Islands.

SCOTLAND.—H. J. L. Allan, Mosscastle, West Linton, Midlothian.

WALES.—C. H. L. Darby, Harwin, Ty-Gwyn Road, Cardiff.

WOMEN'S S.R.A.—Mrs. P. Jackson, 9 Lansdown, Boxgrove Road, Guildford, Surrey.

OTHER SQUASH-PLAYING COUNTRIES

Aden	Greece	Nigeria
Argentina	Guyana	Norway
Bahamas	Hong Kong	Rhodesia
Bahrein	Israel	Sudan
Belgium	Jamaica	Sweden
Bermuda	Japan	Switzerland
Brazil	Kenya	Tanzania
Ceylon	Kuwait	Thailand
Denmark	Malaysia	Trinidad
France	Malta	Uganda
Germany	Mauritius	Zambia
Gibraltar	Netherlands	

(N.B. A different form of squash rackets is played in Canada and the United States of America.)

COACHES

Details of coaches and coaching schemes can be obtained from national associations or from the secretary of the International S.R.F.